To Deane C. Da[...] [who has been] kind and just to me in one of the darkest hours of my life and who has been a valued friend through these many years.

Norris Cotton

WITHDRAWN

IN THE SENATE

Portrait of Senator Cotton by George Augusta;
from the State House, Concord, New Hampshire

IN THE SENATE

Amidst the Conflict and the Turmoil

By

Norris Cotton

United States Senator
from New Hampshire
1954-1975

Dodd, Mead & Company

New York

1 2 3 4 5 6 7 8 9 10

ECL:3

Library of Congress Cataloging in Publication Data

Cotton, Norris.
  In the Senate.

  Includes index.
  1. Cotton, Norris. 2. Legislators—United States—
Biography. 3. United States. Congress. Senate—
Biography. 4. United States—Politics and government—
20th century. I. Title.
E748.C867A34   328.73'092'4 [B]   78—1934
ISBN 0—396—07571—1

Preface

ONE would almost need to be gifted with the "tongues of men and of angel. to convey even a faint impression of the romance of the American Congress, its high moments and its low moments, its sidelights, and the amazing individuals it has numbered in its ranks. Certainly, I do not qualify either as an historian or a writer. Nevertheless, I have an irresistible impulse to record some of the scenes and persons that crowd my memory, as well as some of the knowledge I had an opportunity to gain of customs and practices, trends and developments in our national legislature.

"History," a cynic once remarked, "is usually the story of something that never happened, written by a man who wasn't there." At least, whatever else may be said, I was there—eight years in the House of Representatives and twenty years in the Senate. The bulk of my narrative will be from the viewpoint of a senator.

The first hurdle in my approach to doing this book was the selection of a title. To me this seemed to be of prime importance, although I have since learned that experienced authors usually wait until their manuscript is finished and then select a title appropriate to its contents. Little did I realize the rocky road I was to travel before an acceptable title could be found. While I was still in the Senate, but planning my retirement and dreaming about the book I would write, I was sure of only one thing; and that was its name. The title was to be *If Men*

Were Angels. These words were taken from the observations of James Madison in the "Federalist Papers": "If men were angels, no government would be necessary. If angels were to govern men, neither external nor internal controls on government would be necessary. In framing a government which is to be administered by men over men, the great difficulty lies in this: you must first enable the government to control the governed; and in the next place oblige it to control itself."

As soon as I completed my move from Washington back to New Hampshire, I prepared a tentative outline and began dictating my opening chapters. Then, like a bolt from the blue, I learned that Senator James Buckley of New York had just published a book with that exact title. This was a real setback to a beginner planning his first book. It left me like a ship without a rudder. For some psychological reason, I could not go on with the project until I had found a satisfactory substitute for my pet title.

One of my favorite quotations has long been the words used by Mr. Justice Holmes in referring to the many legal decisions associated with his long career on the Supreme Court: "fragments of my fleece left on the hedges of life." Therefore, I decided the title would be *Fragments of Fleece.* (I rejected "fragments of my fleece," because the book was not to be an autobiography, but impressions of the Congress—even touching on the other branches of government, and including the activities and contributions of many.) I went forward with my writing and ultimately finished the text. Then came my second shock.

One morning a good friend of many years, who was thoroughly familiar with my undertaking and had closely followed the book's progress over a period of many, many months, walked into my office with a broad grin. He handed me a volume he had just stumbled upon while browsing through a bookstore. It was a collection of articles by Dean Acheson, and—sure enough—it was entitled *Fragments of My Fleece.* At that point I threw up my hands and abandoned any hope of finding a name for my book that would be catchy enough to pique the reader's curiosity and at the same time be appropriate to its coverage. Instead, in a measure, I "passed the buck" to the publishers and their editor, looking to them to give a name to the foundling.

Their recommendation was that we make use of a phrase of my own, taken from the manuscript itself, as part of the title ("amidst the conflict and the turmoil") and that the whole indicate plainly, without frills, what the book is about—a New England Yankee's impressions and recollections drawn from his years of service in the United States Senate—thus providing a direct representation of the book's contents, which is, of course, the honest way of labeling any product that is offered to the public.

Contents

IN THE SENATE

CHAPTER

I

Fifty Years of Change

> There is a certain relief in change, even though it be
> from bad to worse; as I have found in traveling in a
> stage-coach, that it is often a comfort to shift one's
> position and be bruised in a new place.
>
> —*Washington Irving*

STRANGELY enough, I can probably assert without fear of contradiction that my personal and intimate knowledge of the Senate of the United States spans more years than does that of any living member or former member of that body. This is true even though there still remain in the Senate a few who outranked me in length of service at the time of my retirement.

My experience with the Senate dates back to 1925, when I became a clerk to the Committee on Post Offices and Post Roads by appointment of its chairman, Senator George H. Moses of New Hampshire. As such, one of my tasks was to submit the nominations for postmasters, which came to us from the White House almost daily, to the senators from the respective states, for them to mark their approval or objection. Thus, I had personal contact with every member of the Senate in those days of long ago. My duties gave me the privilege of the floor at all times, and I spent many hours listening to the debates—sometimes to the detriment of my work as a student at George Washington University Law School.

In those days Washington was just a sleepy, overgrown southern town. Old brick and musty wooden buildings, strewn haphazardly along its avenues, had not yet been replaced by the present massive

1

edifices of marble and granite. Visitors were few, and native Washingtonians viewed the minions of government with lofty indifference. Even President Calvin Coolidge, who loved to stroll up F Street window-shopping, attended by but a single Secret Service man, was accorded hardly a passing glance.

Capitol Hill was almost an ivory tower, in which senators led a sheltered, leisurely existence, their tranquility rarely disturbed by probing letters, fact-finding constituents, or crusading delegations. (One penny-pinching bachelor senator saved the cost of a hotel room by setting up a bed behind a screen in his office, and he got away with it for several months.)

Everything has changed so incredibly that looking back on it today is almost like reading a Thackeray novel. The nation's population has doubled. Radio and television have made people more conscious of their government. The jet plane, the bus, and above all, the family automobile have made Washington a mecca for tourists who flock through the Capitol—sometimes as many as 20,000 a day. Huge concentrations of population have created problems beyond the power of local communities to solve and made people dependent on their federal government even for the water they drink and the air they breathe. Two World Wars, with their resulting regimentation and controls, have put the government in everybody's hair.

Senator Moses, who gave me my committee job in 1925, was not only one of the senate's seniors, but its president pro tempore and a national figure. Yet one secretary and two stenographers were quite adequate to handle his mail and to conduct the other business of his office. Today senatorial staffs are determined by the population of the states involved. A senator from New York or California requires a personal staff of thirty to forty-five people just to deal with the problems of constituents and to handle the bulging sacks of mail delivered daily to his office. A senator from a small state like New Hampshire requires at least a dozen.

In the 1920s a senator's job was strictly part-time. Sessions began in December and never ran into midsummer. (There was no air conditioning then!) Thus, senators spent more than half their time at home, where they engaged in their regular vocations. More important, they remained a part of their home communities and never lost touch with their people. Today it is a full-time job in Washington, with at best only a few weeks at home. No matter how many flying trips they make to their states, senators can personally be in contact with only a small segment of the people, and the rest rarely see them. Unlike the House, debate is rarely limited, so senators can't know in advance when crucial votes are coming. Whenever they take a chance and absent themselves, they are liable to be caught off base.

A senator's work today is infinitely more challenging than in the leisurely days of the twenties. The heat of controversy, the force of public pressure, the spur of criticism, the stimulation of clashing opinions in the Senate and at home make a senator's job more difficult, but at the same time they release the last drop of adrenalin and add to the zest of living.

A substantial number of today's senators tend to be brisk, efficient specialists drawn from many fields. Gone are the swallow-tailed coats and flowing locks. Gone are the floods of classic oratory; speeches are now much more likely to be crisp and to the point—and often highly technical. To be sure, although their ranks are dwindling, there still remains a remnant of the old-time marathon orators. These love the sound of their own voices, and they indulge in long hours of oratory, even to an empty Senate and empty galleries. The late Senator Wayne Morse was a good example of this type. So, in a measure, was Hubert Humphrey. Make no mistake, however, Humphrey was no "windbag." He had one of the sharpest minds in the Senate, but he was simply unable to stem the flow of words.

A deep feeling of nostalgia envelops me when I recall the senators of more than fifty years ago. No doubt their personalities and abilities were magnified in the eyes of an impressionable youth of twenty-five. Quite likely they did not excel, or perhaps even equal, those with whom I served in later years or the young men who have been moving into the "seats of the mighty" since I left. Indeed, those towering figures of the twenties might well find difficulty in coping with the complexities of the 1970s. Perhaps they were no abler than their present-day successors, but they were certainly shaped in a different mold. There was less uniformity; they were more individualistic and their qualities, traits, and characteristics stood out in bold relief. They bridged the gap between the Senate of Webster, Clay, and Calhoun and the Senate of today.

It is even more nostalgic when, in memory, I listen again to the varied accents that then still greeted the ears of the Senate. America had not yet become a conglomerate. The covered wagons of the pioneers had ceased to roll. Automobiles were in their infancy. The mobile home was in the far future. There were railroads but few airlines; and the vast majority of Americans were homebodies rather than migrants. Thus, on the Senate floor one heard the nasal twang of old New England (Moses of New Hampshire, Dillingham of Vermont, Fernald of Maine, and Brandegee of Connecticut all talked through their noses, as did Calvin Coolidge). The southern drawl was much in evidence. Some southern senators still speak with a slight accent, but in those days you could cut it with a knife. Jim Watson of Indiana, Medill McCormick of Illinois, Simeon Fess of Ohio, Cummins of Iowa, as well as Curtis and Capper of Kansas employed the flat tones of the Midwest (this was not quite true of Vice President Curtis—he was part Indian). Far-western senators used the jargon of the ranch. (Stanfield of Oregon and Peter Norbeck of South Dakota were both so bow-legged from years in the saddle that they were almost grotesque in the gray-striped trousers and morning coats of formal wear.)

As a country lad fresh from the hills of New Hampshire, I studied those senators with fascination. Few, if any, of their individual mannerisms, quirks of personality, or even the inflections of their voices escaped my eager observation. Today they are more sharply etched in my memory than many with whom I served from time to time during the last twenty of those years spent as a senator myself. As age draws on, youthful memories remain the sharpest, and I could easily devote considerable space to depicting those senators of the 1920s. A few of the outstanding ones are well worth recalling.

My own boss, George Moses, a man of many contradictory traits, was in many respects the most brilliant senator who ever represented New Hampshire, and he merits more than passing attention. The son of a minister, his boyhood was spent in Franklin, New Hampshire. He took both his baccalaureate and Master's degrees at Dartmouth College, where he excelled in modern languages, as well as in his mother tongue. A natural-born linguist, during his life he mastered five and had a reasonable working knowledge of three others. I vividly recall a campaign night when, driving for him in Manchester, I heard him address a crowd at Lafayette Hall in French, another group in West Manchester in German, and then wind up at the city hall in English; and so far as I could observe, he appeared to use all three languages with equal fluency.

Always a stickler for precise grammar and diction, he used to reprimand me sharply for what he called a "slovenly" failure to sound each syllable, such as sliding over the "p" in "New Hampshire." A speech impediment made it difficult for me to sound my "r"s. Hurrying from his committee office when the Senate adjourned, he would spy me at my desk, stop in his tracks, and summon me into his office —where he would make me rapidly recite "Around the rugged rock the ragged rascal ran."

Moses was truly a master of words. Fresh out of college, he began as a reporter for the *Concord Monitor,* and years later became its owner and publisher. With his natural aptitude for languages and his years of writing, he acquired a vocabulary more varied and complete than any person I have ever known. Many of his editorials were almost classics, and they were frequently quoted by the great metropolitan newspapers of the nation.

President Taft appointed him minister to Greece, where he served with distinction, and upon his return to this country, he was elected in 1918 to the U.S. Senate to fill out the unexpired term of Senator Jacob H. Gallinger. As far as the history of the last hundred years discloses, he was the only senator ever to be chosen president pro tempore who was not the most senior senator of the party in control.

He spoke as he wrote, with an imagination that added glitter to many dry subjects. The chief political issue between the parties at that period was free trade or a protective tariff—not a subject to cause heartthrobs. Yet he was able to make it come alive:

> Did you ever stop to think that Mary, Queen of Scots, never enjoyed the luxury of running water in the Holyrood Palace; that her great rival, Queen Elizabeth, never knew the exquisite sensation of munching a superb Huyler's chocolate; that Madame de Maintenon never swathed her lovely figure in a Royal Worcester corset; or that Cleopatra never knew what it was to grab up a party-line telephone and give Marc Antony a ring for a date? Did you ever stop to think that Julius Caesar, in all his glory, never rode in a flivver—and yet these, my friends, are the commonplaces of the American standard of living as guaranteed by a Republican protective tariff.

His capacity for tenderness (which he strove to conceal) is revealed in his brief eulogy at the death of his friend, Senator Overman of North Carolina:

> He was then the beau ideal of a Senator—in appearance and in all the qualities of mind and soul which equip men for service here. With a toga upon his rugged shoulders and a fillet around his snow-white locks, he could have stepped back through the ages and walked the Pretorian pavements on terms of complete equality with any senator of ancient Rome. It was but natural that the tremendous tasks which he was then laying down should have left their mark upon him, and that his slackening powers should have found thereafter only those occasional bursts of fiery zeal with which he sometimes roused himself to action which electrified the Senate. He was passing into the evening of his life—an evening destined to be long and golden, warmed with color of an autumn day. He was surrounded by the solicitude of an adoring family—and we shared that solicitude with them. He fell to sleep and we saw him laid to his rest, our grief tempered by the reflection that we had been privi' leged to know him and to love him.

The world never saw, nor does history record, the human, compassionate side of George Moses. This was his fault. To the world he gave the impression of a cynical, sarcastic, brilliant individual with a biting tongue. In later years, when I was more mature, I came to realize that he enjoyed that role—indeed, that he almost reveled in it. His wit was sharp as a rapier and he could not resist uttering a witticism, no matter how cutting. Years later my Senate colleagues from the West used to say of him, "Oh, yes, Moses was the man who called us westerners 'sons of the wild jackass.'" (Actually, the expression was a quote from the Old Testament.) And he alienated the temperance people by calling the Volstead Act a "jackass statute." (What he really said was that under the definitions of the Volstead Act "buttermilk is an intoxicating beverage and that makes it a jackass statute.") Then, when Moses told newsmen that President Wilson had suffered a stroke, Admiral Grayson, the president's physician, indignantly demanded to know when Moses had qualified as a doctor. "The same day Grayson qualified as an admiral," was Moses' reply.

Influential and highly respected southerners of that period were men like Joseph T. Robinson of Arkansas, minority leader of the Senate; Oscar W. Underwood of Alabama, loyally supported by the South for president; Walter F. George of Georgia; and Pat Harrison of Mississippi. There were others who posed and postured as "professional southerners," and conspicuous among them was Tom Heflin of Alabama.

A huge man, both tall and portly, with red hair and a ruddy complexion, Heflin always wore the traditional Prince Albert coat and white vest. An unreconstructed rebel and racist, gifted with powerful lungs, he was constantly heard ranting for "white supremacy" and against Roman Catholics, who, he claimed, were plotting to take over the government. (Legend had it that while Heflin was a congressman, a half-intoxicated black spoke to him slightingly, whereupon Heflin drew a pistol and shot him. The black recovered, the police ignored the incident, and Alabama promptly promoted Heflin to the U.S. Senate.) He was never taken seriously. In fact, when he frequently charged that the Pope was seeking to control America, Catholic senators like David I. Walsh of Massachusetts used to laugh themselves sick. (Legend also had it that someone in the Democratic National Committee inadvertently assigned Heflin to speak at a

Democratic state convention in Massachusetts. Senator Walsh received him courteously at Boston, as a senatorial colleague, and took him into the lobby of Young's Hotel to await the hour for presenting him to the convention. The Holy Name Society happened also to be holding a convention in the city, and its members were forming a parade, marching four abreast around Young's Hotel, while other units were marshaled and preparing to join them. Heflin watched this seemingly endless procession with ever-increasing apprehension, until he finally burst out to Walsh, "I didn't know there were so many Catholics in the world." To which Walsh replied, "Hell, Tom, these are just the ones who don't swear.")

Another southern senator of whom I have vivid memories was John Sharp Williams of Mississippi. He represented to the nth degree the aristocrats who dominated the South when segregation was the accepted way of life and civil rights had never been heard of, when the scars of Reconstruction were still fresh and white supremacy was unchallenged. The southern gentlemen I observed in the Senate a half-century ago maintained a paternal attitude toward blacks. For them as individuals, they had a certain affection and solicitude; but as a race they kept them in servitude, refusing them opportunities for education and advancement, and they regarded them as irresponsible children, incapable of fending for themselves or of attaining full stature as human beings or equality as citizens.

A striking manifestation of this attitude was the southern senators' championship of prohibition. Many, if not most, of them had to have their mint juleps and hot toddies, but they stoutly upheld prohibition because, they said, "the Negroes could not be trusted to handle liquor."

John Sharp Williams was an extreme example of this stance. He imbibed freely himself, but defended prohibition with all his might. One day he was delivering an eloquent speech for prohibition. Another senator, asking him to yield for a question, inquired if the senator from Mississippi were a teetotaler. Instantly Williams replied, "The senator knows full well that I am an habitual drinker, but I will say to the senator that I am not a slave to the habit. In fact, on one occasion I went six months without a single drink—and, Mr. President, I must say that I never had one original thought during that whole period."

For many years the men of the South, though very much in the minority, wielded an influence far beyond their numerical strength, because the southern custom was to keep the same senators in office until they exceeded senators from all other sections of the country in seniority. Thus, when the Democrats came into power, first under Wilson and later with FDR, the chairman of nearly every powerful committee was from the South.

When, in 1954, I entered the Senate as a member of that body, there remained only two senators whom I had watched as a staffer more than a quarter-century before. One was Senator George of Georgia, powerful chairman of the Committee on Foreign Relations (whom Franklin D. Roosevelt had tried in vain to purge because of his coolness toward the New Deal). However, the rising power of Governor Talmadge was to prove too much for Senator George and forced him into retirement two years later. The other was Senator Neely of West Virginia, whom I recall as one of the most fierce and flowery of the Senate's southern orators. The years, I found, had taken away none of his fire. He devoted time each day for reading Shakespeare and other great works of literature, to increase his vocabulary and refine his eloquence. It was rumored that he even practiced his speeches before a mirror. Each year on the anniversary of one of the southern victories in the Civil War, he would rise and deliver a speech on the glories of the South.

As a young man I had a quick and retentive memory (I do not have now), so I never forgot the opening volleys of that annual speech by Senator Neeley—which he was still delivering, I found, after thirty years:

> When God made Dixie He must have been in a particularly happy frame of mind, for with one gesture of His generous hand He unfurled a thousand square miles of blue sky like a scroll from the Ohio to the Gulf and from ocean to ocean. He lighted it with the same smiling sun that shed its brilliant rays over cultured Athens in the

Golden Age of Pericles, and shone over happy Italy when Horace sang of the field and of the vine. He peopled it with a race whose womanhood is as pure as the pond lily's spotless leaf, and whose manhood love the land because it is their own, and scorn to give another reason why; who would shake hands with a king upon his throne and count it a kindness to His Majesty. . . .

But perhaps the most striking figure in those early days was William E. Borah of Idaho, one of the few senators whose name is still remembered years after his death. As a young lawyer in Boise, his first political ventures were failures. He was defeated first as a candidate for the national House and later for the U.S. Senate. Fame and success came to him, however, after his fearless and victorious fight in two famous cases. The first involved the Coeur d'Alene mining riots, when a thousand members of the miners' union destroyed two mines and killed two men. Local authorities, fearful of the power of the union which dominated the county, refused to act. Borah, appointed special prosecutor, convicted the murderers, despite attacks and threats against his life. To this day his powerful argument to the jury is pointed to as one of the most famous jury speeches of our history. Then, in 1907, he convicted the officials of the Western Federation of Miners, charged with bringing about the assassination of Governor Steunenburg. That year he was elected to the U.S. Senate, and he was reelected throughout the remainder of his life.

Although he had fought vicious and violent labor unions in Idaho, he was not a conservative. In fact, by nature and temperament he was a "lone wolf" who never identified himself with either the Populist liberals in the Senate, such as La Follette and Brookhart, or the regular Republican organization. He loved to espouse unpopular and lost causes, and for years he fought a hopeless battle against the overwhelming majority, on both sides of the Senate, seeking recognition of the Soviet regime in Russia—in that day usually called the "Bolsheviks." Despite the fact that he was a Republican, he was a thorn in the side of every Republican president—which led to Calvin Coolidge's famous remark, on being told that Borah took his exercise each morning by riding in Rock Creek Park: "I can't understand that," said

Coolidge. "How can be bring himself to go the same way the horse is going?"

Finally, one general observation concerning the senators of those days of long ago, from the standpoint of a youthful staffer. As I have explained, the duties of my clerkship compelled me to approach all the senators with nominations for postmasters (a method long since discarded; nowadays such communications are mailed to the senators' offices and handled through their assistants). If a bunch of twenty-five postmasters' nominations came up from the White House on a Monday and a similar package later in the week, I could not let any grass grow under my feet in reaching the fifteen or twenty senators whose states would be involved in each group of nominations. Otherwise they would pile up, and members would soon be asking what had happened to them.

Then as now, senators would rush onto the floor, respond to roll calls, and immediately disappear back into their committees or elsewhere. That meant I had to act swiftly, approaching them when they were busy or in conversation, wait until they had concluded or at least paused, and then thrust the nominations before their faces, with the request that they mark their approval or objection. This could be very irritating to them, but it had to be done.

Now, here is an interesting fact. There was a group of "old war horses" in the Senate widely noted as caustic debaters. Among them were senators like Borah, Hiram Johnson of California, James A. Reed of Missouri, the senior La Follette of Wisconsin, Watson of Indiana, George W. Norris of Nebraska—to name a few. These men were blunt and ruthless when battling with each other. But, almost without exception, they were surprisingly kind and patient when approached by an underling in the performance of his duty. On the other hand, many senators who appeared gentle and scrupulously courteous when debating with their colleagues were instantly annoyed when I had to approach them, and they would almost bite my head off. In other words, they were smooth with their equals, but overbearing with staffers who had to take it, while those who were belligerent with their equals were considerate of their inferiors who could not answer back. I had many a humiliating moment and shall never forget that peculiar contradictory trait. (It was fresh in my memory when I myself became a senator, and I tried never to speak sharply to committee clerks and others.)

So much for the olden days. A beautiful illustration of the difference between the old Senate and the new is a tidbit from *Reader's Digest*. A mother and her teenage daughter were watching a 1930s film on television. As it concluded, with the usual romantic embrace of that era, the daughter observed, "Gosh, Mom, your movies ended where ours begin."

CHAPTER

II

Apprenticeship in the House of Representatives

*If you keep your mind sufficiently open, people
will throw a lot of rubbish into it.*
—William A. Orton

IN 1928, having passed the bar and said goodbye to Washington, I had no real thought or expectation of ever seeing the U.S. Senate again, except perhaps as a visitor to its gallery. For nearly twenty years I devoted myself to the law in New Hampshire, first gaining some experience working for a law firm in Concord, and then striking out for myself at Lebanon, in my native county of Grafton, ultimately forming the law firm of Cotton, Tesreau & Stebbins of that city. My only political offices were ones connected with my profession; I was elected as county attorney and subsequently served as justice of the municipal court of Lebanon by appointment of the governor.

Later I became a member of the state legislature, not because of any particular political ambition, but rather to familiarize myself with the state's problems and to expand my personal and professional contacts. I served as majority floor leader under the speakership of Sherman Adams, and when he moved on to Congress, I succeeded him as speaker. Then came an unexpected development that changed the whole course of my life.

Adams, after two years, gave up his congressional seat and returned to New Hampshire to run for governor. That left the seat in Congress up for grabs, and I decided to run for it. Perhaps I was partly motivated by a subconscious yen to return to Capitol Hill. At any rate, I succeeded in being nominated and elected.

Of course, I was entering into a far different world from the one I had known. It was a far cry from being a Senate committee clerk in the 1920s to being a member of the national House of Representatives in the late forties. Many of the changes described in the previous chapter had taken place, and the House of Representatives, because of its size, its composition, its rules and procedures is far different from the Senate—particularly the Senate for which I had worked two decades earlier. Nevertheless, service in the House affords a good apprenticeship for service in the Senate, and the unforgettable lessons learned by a freshman congressman will stand him in good stead no matter how long he may serve in either body.

It is during the early days that a new member of Congress catches his first sight of the ever-unfolding panorama of Washington's official life. He also sustains for the first time the impact of the people, especially the young people, constantly thronging the halls of Congress to register their approval or disapproval—usually the latter—of their government. It is then that he begins to deal with the flow of mail from constitutents, which swells into a river and continues to flow throughout his service.

Those who staff the committees of Congress study legislation, draft amendments, and prepare analyses of bills for the information of the members themselves. They are, in fact, legislative technicians. Their work is important and requires skill, but it gives them not even an inkling of the problems of senators and congressmen who must constantly respond to the demands of thousands of constituents.

In recent years, I find myself both interested in and a bit amused by my own first impressions as a freshman congressman, as related to my home folks in New Hampshire in the earliest of my "Reports" to them. Others may also find interest and amusement, remembering these are the words of a new—a very new—congressman:

Everything that Congress does, or does not do, affects us all. Congress can raise or lower the price of ham and eggs—your

payroll or your pay check—build a road or a dam—divert a river—
affect the schools . . . the health . . . or the housing in your local
community.

Congress can declare peace or war. It can even set your watch.
Congress is as local as the City Hall or the County Court House,
and as national as big league baseball.

The day of President Truman's inauguration and the day preceding it apparently left deep impressions upon me:

On Wednesday, Washington was invaded by an aggregation of
demonstrators who called themselves a "Freedom Crusade." They
tramped through the corridors looking at the portraits and statues
of historical figures, with a sneer on their faces, and as we members
edged furtively into our offices, we heard mutters about "flag
wavers," "servants of privilege," "political hacks," and similar flat-
tering expressions.

The group that called on me demanded that the trials of the
Communists in New York be stopped, that we abolish the Un-
American Activities Committee, and reduce the Armed Forces.
They were young folks (twenty-year-old college students) and
talked about the way we all did when we were in college; the world
was all wrong, capitalism was wrong, in fact there was nothing
much right about the country. I could plainly see I was one of the
things that was wrong.

After they left, I could still hear them tramping the corridors.
I began to read my mail which consisted of letters demanding that
I vote for this or that "or else." I began to have qualms and doubts,
and did not feel like a statesman.

Wednesday was a dark, rainy, dismal day.

* * *

Thursday was a bright, clear, beautiful day and another and far
greater army descended upon Washington. They were a different
breed altogether. In the morning I watched them troop past my hotel, which is near the station, and mill around the Capitol grounds.
They were not state leaders and highbrows who ordinarily come to
inaugurations (twenty-three thousand rooms in Washington went
untenanted). They thronged in on the special trains and brought

their lunches with them to eat on the grounds. They were the "little folks" who had elected the man whom the little folks like. Many of the women carried babies in their arms. There were no sneers and no sullen looks. It was their Capitol, their city, and their country, and they liked it.

The President did not disappoint them. He spoke simply and sincerely about peace abroad, prosperity at home, and a strong America. I did not care for his message to Congress last week, but I liked his inaugural speech. It showed that even though like the rest of us he may be misguided at times, his heart is in the right place. It was the simple creed of an honest American. When it was over and the last band had marched by, the folks went back to the station and climbed on the trains, leaving the Capitol grounds covered with lunch boxes and paper bags.

I went back to my office with renewed hope. I felt like a statesman again and wanted a part in the job that is to be done. The lofty phrases of a speech were already beginning to form in my mind and I decided it was pretty grand to be your Congressman.

Then I opened my first letter. It said that in New Hampshire they are now selling dressed chickens without the giblets. There ought to be a law against it. Let him know by return mail what I was going to do about it, and get busy "or else."

It's a great life here.

I had, in fact, been forewarned. Shortly after I was elected, but before going to Washington, I called on an aged ex-congressman whom I had known and respected for years. It was not long before his death and physically he was extremely feeble. There was nothing feeble about his mind, however. He was alert and keenly interested in what was going on in the world. You will probably anticipate that I am about to tell you how this dear old man put his hand on my shoulder and gave me inspiring counsel that lingered with me like a benediction. Not so. He sat propped up in bed, with a newspaper in his lap, chewing on a cigar, and said something like this: "Boy, you are young and starting a career in Congress. I'm an old man about to kick off, but I'm not sure I envy you. This government has grown so big that you'll find yourself buried by a mass of problems you have never even heard about, and it will be months, if not years, before you begin to catch a glimmer of light. I'll give you just one piece of advice. If you keep your damn mouth shut, they won't realize how little you know."

How right he was! But he didn't tell me the worst. It is not so much the size and complications of government that baffle a new congressman, as it is the fact that he finds himself constantly handcuffed by the legislative process. He rarely has the opportunity to vote for what he wants, but nearly always has to take the lesser of two evils—and then try to explain the whys and wherefores to his constituents. Thus, during one fateful month, I voted for a compulsory Selective Service bill I disliked, a tax bill I detested, and a price-and-wage-control bill I abominated.

It is wonderful to go to Washington with a nice set of ready-made principles and theories tucked neatly in one's mental traveling bag, and with a moral code all polished and shining. But fitting these principles to reality is not so easy. They go in like an ill-fitting set of false teeth. It is not that one surrenders one's principles, but one is constantly compelled to settle for the best of several unsatisfactory substitutes. As Senator Ralph Flanders once put it, in his down-to-earth Vermont way, "The time comes when you have to forget principle and just vote for what is right."

Cunning artifices and clever juggling by an adroit leadership too frequently put the earnest young member right behind the eight ball. From long experience, veteran legislators have mastered the art of using the rules of the House as a weapon to enforce their will, and a deadly weapon it is in their hands. They use tactics too devious to describe in detail. Some of these may have been remedied by rule changes in the years since I served in the House, but there surely are plenty left. One favorite device in my day was called "suspensions."

In the more leisurely days of the opening months of a session of Congress, bills come in under a regular rule, and the membership can amend, revise, and revamp to their heart's content (except tax bills). However, as time presses and the session's end draws near, it is a new ball game. A motion is made to "suspend the rules and pass the bill"— all in one fell swoop. The debate, usually limited to forty minutes, is controlled by top members of the committee sponsoring the bill, and they are seasoned quarterbacks. The bill cannot be amended or altered one iota. The House must take it or leave it—and quick!

It is not by chance that we dawdle along through the early part of a session. The leadership can say, in the famous words of FDR, "we planned it that way." If they let controversial measures pile up, and then shoot them into the House in the closing days, they can usually get their own way. It is an almost sure-fire scheme, with a booby trap hidden in nearly every bill. The strategy is very simple. If the leaders want to force through an unpopular bill, they cement it to an urgently needed measure for which everybody is clamoring. The House must swallow the bitter with the sweet. If, on the other hand, they want to scuttle a bill, they insert in it some feature so obnoxious and abhorrent that the necessary two-thirds vote to suspend the rules cannot be obtained. Simple, isn't it? And it works like a charm.

An instance of this snide maneuvering was a bill increasing old-age benefits under Social Security. The majority leadership, which controls the House calendar, did not want this bill passed in that particular session of Congress. They wanted to save it for the next session, which came just before a presidential election. So it was brought in at the last minute under a "suspension," and then sinister whispers were circulated that it contained "socialized medicine." That was tommy-rot; it merely permitted examinations by government doctors of applicants claiming total disability, exactly as is done by the Veterans Administration. Calling that socialized medicine was as ridiculous as calling a man's home a zoo because he keeps a dog. But the damage was done. The powerful sentiment against socialized medicine was aroused. A two-thirds vote could not be obtained, and the impoverished old people (about whom politicians shed so many tears) had to wait until the next session.

Now with situations as complicated as these, and with so many hidden factors and concealed motives, it is mighty easy for the individual member, particularly in his early years, to make mistakes; and of course he does. I will mention a couple of my own, as examples of the pitfalls into which a representative may fall, the motives that cause his errors, the punishment that may follow, and the bitter lessons he learns —and never forgets.

Let me describe the worst one first—the worst because it was *not* just an honest mistake of judgment, although I succeeded in rationalizing my action to myself at that time. Actually, I yielded to political expediency and suffered from it more, politically, than from any other act in all my years in Washington. It seems almost funny to think of it now, but I assure you it was not funny then; and a real principle is involved which is not to be taken lightly.

Liquor may cause the downfall of some men. Feminine wiles may shatter the resistance of others. Monetary greed may be the Waterloo of many. My own besetting sin was oleomargarine. I had hardly been on the Committee on Agriculture long enough to get my seat warm when the famous "Oleo Bill" descended upon me like a bolt from the blue. It did not seem like a thunderbolt at first, and I had no idea how long its results would abide with me or how deep would be its scars.

I had some vague knowledge that the farmers disliked the sale of butter substitutes and that it had been a subject of controversy in some state legislatures, as well as in the Congress. But little did I realize how strong and venomous were the feelings on this issue or the political dynamite it contained. The federal government had long collected a margarine tax which, in the case of margarine colored to resemble butter, was so heavy as to be prohibitive. The proposed new bill would have removed the special federal tax on colored oleo. Frankly, my first impression was that the tax was unsound and unjust. If oleomargarine were impure or detrimental to the health, its sale should be prohibited under the Pure Food and Drug Act. If it were not harmful, people should be allowed to have it if they wanted it. In other words, plainly label each package of butter and each package of oleo, let each product stand on its own feet, and allow the consumers to have their choice. How often first impressions are correct, and how happy I would have been if I had stuck to mine!

Now comes the story of the gradual disintegration of the good resolutions of a new and innocent congressman. Almost every man who sat on the Republican side of the Committee on Agriculture represented a northern dairy district. There were only two or three of us, all freshmen, who came from consumer districts that had as many factories as cows. Most of the men on the Democratic side of the committee came from southern agricultural districts that had few dairy herds, but were large producers of cotton and peanuts. Cottonseed oil and peanut oil go into margarine. Powerful motives involving both partisanship and sectionalism were massed on both sides of this question. From the moment the hearings on the bill began, the senior members on our side of the committee were working on the two or three new and doubtful members, of which I was one. We were told that if we took away the defenses that protected the dairy farmer from the competition of butter substitutes, the dairy industry would be ruined. It was pointed out to us that the northern agricultural states and districts were the bulwarks of the Republican party and that if the first Republican Congress in many years took away this tax, which had been preserved for more than half a century, the farmers would never forgive us—and this would cause our defeat in the coming presidential election.

It was impressed upon us that a vote for the bill was a vote to reverse the outcome of Civil War and to put the heel of the rich southern cotton planters upon the neck of the poor Yankee dairymen. Senior members who earlier had seemed scarcely aware of our existence paid us much attention, invited us youngsters to lunch and showered kindnesses upon us. One or two of them, very tactfully and in an indirect manner, reminded us that we were, of course, expected to play on the team and stand by our colleagues on the committee if we were to have their support, if and when we needed something badly for our own districts. Moreover, the farm organizations in my home state began to show interest in this matter, and I was the recipient of showers of telegrams and letters (I was still too "green" to evaluate properly a storm of mail inspired by a national organization). One executive actually made a trip to Washington to urge me to stand firm for the farmers. When I still showed signs of doubt and mentioned the problems of the housewife, the most telling argument (or at least the best alibi of all) was brought forth. My own state of New Hampshire had a law that barred the manufacture, importation, or sale of colored margarine. Accordingly, if the bill passed, the New Hampshire housewife still could not get her yellow spread, unless our own legislature repealed the state law. Behold: if I voted for the bill I was flying in the face of the aggregate wisdom of the New Hampshire legislature, which for years had completely banned yellow margarine. So, I could very easily extend a helping hand to my colleagues, without doing one bit of harm to any housewife in my home state.

The impact of all this persuasion was overwhelming. I yielded completely. Not only did I capitulate, as did two or three of my fellow freshmen who had also had misgivings, but I even succeeded in convincing myself that my new position was sound and that I had been mistaken in my first impression. It would have been bad enough had I just voted against the tax-repeal bill, but I went further than that. I joined my colleagues on the Republican side of the committee in voting to postpone all action upon it until another session of Congress. In other words, we buried it in committee, so the House would not have a chance to vote on it. Of course, there were extenuating circumstances for my action. In a sense I was trying, or thought I was trying, to do what was wise or best, for certainly there were no motives of personal gain in my decision, except perhaps the desire to win the good will of my congressional associates. I was a new member, inclined to be overawed by the dignity and prestige of my seniors. I appreciated then, as I still do, that a certain amount of party discipline is necessary; that if we are effectively to maintain the two-party system, individuals must, of necessity, yield on minor matters that do not involve their basic principles or their integrity, in the interests of concerted action.

All this was so much eyewash. The fact remained that restricting the use of oleo by means of a federal tax is clearly repugnant to the whole theory of our government and, furthermore, a weak reed to be leaned upon by the farmer. I was wrong in the course I pursued and, deep in my heart, I knew it.

The punishment was swift and sure. There must be an immutable law underlying politics and legislative actions (just as it underlies life in general), because I have observed that punishment usually follows when a legislator actually surrenders principle for what appears to be expediency.

In this instance, here is what happened. When the action of seventeen members of our committee in pigeonholing the Oleo Bill became known, a wave of indignation swept over the entire country. To be sure, the same action had been taking place for several successive Congresses before this one, but times were different then. When our committee acted, the cost of living had been mounting by leaps and bounds. Housewives everywhere were struggling with their budgets, and butter was one of the high-priced commodities. They wanted oleo, and they wanted *yellow* oleo. They did not want white, pasty stuff they had to color and mix up themselves. The margarine companies had run a national campaign of advertising to whet consumer appetites for the commodity and had made them aware of its money-saving advantages. Now, finding that a bunch of congressmen had coolly sidetracked this measure, they rose up in fury.

Most of the other members who had so voted came from dairy districts, and they were not greatly affected, but my district was not predominantly a dairy district—a fact I discovered right quick! Housewives flooded me with letters. Newspapers blistered me in editorials. Worse yet, I had little support from such dairy farmers as there were in my district, because few of them produced butter; most of them shipped their milk to the Boston fluid-milk market—and a surprising number of them used oleo on their own tables.

Public pressure was so great that more than the necessary 218 congressmen (more than half the House) signed what is known as a "discharge petition," forcing the committee to report the bill, which the House promptly passed. This did not relieve my situation, however. The grocers, consumers, and housewives in my district were out for my scalp. It was useless to talk to them about the southern cottonseed interests or the midwestern soybean growers or the oleo manufacturers or any other group having selfish interests in the measure. Nor was it of any avail to point out that they could not possibly benefit from passage of the bill anyway, because New Hampshire state law still prohibited colored margarine. They turned deaf ears to all this. A bill intended to relax restrictions on their oleo had been scuttled in the Congress by a small group, and their representative was one of that group. Fortunately for me, a year had to elapse before my campaign for reelection, and in the meantime the bill had died in the Senate, so popular indignation had been turned, more or less, toward that body. Nevertheless, when I campaigned for my second term, I was coated with oleo whenever I appeared. My votes on such far-reaching measures as foreign aid, tax reduction, and the Taft-Hartley labor law were rarely mentioned, while in almost every public meeeting some housewife or retail merchant would sail into me about oleomargarine.

I weathered the storm, but I learned my lesson. When I returned for my next term in Congress, I served notice in advance to my colleagues on the committee that I was not helping to pull any more of their chestnuts out of the fire, that my constituents wanted the oleo tax repealed, and more important, I really believed the tax should be repealed—and intended to so vote. Of course, my position with my colleagues on the committee was now much worse than if I had opposed them in the first place. I had made every mistake that could possibly be made in dealing with the issue, and I succeeded, before all was over, in antagonizing both sides of the controversy.

When I faced my conscience honestly, I was forced to recognize that I had been deluding myself and that I had rather weakly allowed myself to be inveigled into voting against my own best judgment. My only course was to admit frankly that I was wrong and try to rectify it.

The incident has been buried with the years and I rarely hear about it nowadays, but the bitter humiliation I experienced when I realized that I had made a fool of myself taught me a lesson. I continued to go along with my party and play on the "team," but when the chips were down and a vote came on any matter in which important principle was involved, I did not again permit myself to cast a vote not consistent with my personal convictions.

Whenever I was tempted to go along with my colleagues on an "I'll scratch your back and you scratch mine" basis, or to vote for some measure to help a friend or because we ought to do something for the "western boys" or the "southern boys" or for the "good of the party"—

in short, whenever I began to feel the gentle pull of political expediency—usually a very distinct taste of oleo in my mouth warned me not to permit myself to be buttered up. It was a costly lesson, but I am inclined to believe that it was worth the price I had to pay. It is a lesson that every congressman must learn sooner or later, and I'm glad that I learned it sooner.

In the story I have recited, I have frankly confessed that I deserved the punishment I received. However, members of Congress frequently suffer from unpopular votes that were cast in good faith. Perhaps the greatest bane of a congressman's existence (next to appointing postmasters) is so-called "pork-barrel legislation." When the bills that carry funds for reclamation, flood control, and improvement of rivers and harbors make their appearance in the House, they are a signal for a mad scramble. There is certainly no "flood control" on oratory, and members go into rhapsodies about the merits of every project from Alabama's Chattahoochee to Oklahoma's Polecat Creek. (Familiar to many are the opening lines of the famous oration by Rankin of Mississippi: "Upon the bosom of the Tombigbee River floats the commerce of the world. . . .") Pork-barrel legislation is one of the worst features of the whole system of federal grants and subsidies, and it is justly condemned.

I have consistently opposed pork-barrel bills, but I must confess that I deserve little credit for doing so. Such opposition has been comparatively easy for me, because few of these plums find their way into New England and, accordingly, rarely has there been any benefit for my own district in these bills. But before condemning representatives from sections who seem always to be promoting these projects, it would be well to remember what these congressmen are up against. In the great river areas, a congressman must be able not only to analyze the mood and temper of his people, but he must, in a sense, be a weather forecaster as well. If for the sake of national economy he dares to oppose a flood-control dam, and if later a flood hits his district, he is a "gone goose." I have seen several able and useful members go out of Congress because of such a vote, honestly and fearlessly cast.

National defense is another realm spotted with mines and booby traps, and full of political dynamite. Actually, every congressman takes his political life in his hands when he deals with defense appropriations, and he should be looking into a crystal ball at all times. This makes it hard to muster votes in the House to make even minor reductions in huge military appropriation bills, and when such is attempted, long-time members warn every newcomer, "Don't touch national defense. You'll be sorry." They point to the political graves of those who have guessed wrong in the past—the men who voted against Selective Service just before World War II; the men who voted against fortifying Guam; the men who voted to cut military appropriations on the eve of Korea. Members shiver at the thought of what will happen to them if they reject one demand of the Pentagon and then an enemy strikes at us somewhere.

When my people were, at last, contentedly spreading their bread thick with oleo, I had acquired other obstacles in running for subsequent reelection. One was my vote on Korean aid. Just before the Korean conflict broke out, the House considered a bill for economic assistance to Korea. There were many objections to it. It provided large sums to develop hydroelectric power and to build industrial plants in South Korea, which when complete would be attractive prizes for the Communists to take over, yet supplied nothing for weapons and military support with which to defend them. This ignored the fact that American diplomats and members of Congress returning from Asia were unanimous in warning that an attack by North Koreans was inevitable.

On the other hand, the bill carried appropriations for food, medicine, technical and scientific advice and assistance, and for much other help that was needed. I felt we had neglected our Asiatic friends and was anxious that we fulfill our obligations to them. Still, I did not like the bill. Furthermore, one of those little "behind-the-scenes" incidents occurred which are never obvious to the public, but which often sway the minds of legislators and sometimes lead them to vote on impulse. An able member of the Foreign Affairs Committee, after speaking for the bill on the floor of the House, went out into the cloakroom. I happened to follow him and overheard him say to a friend, "We have to support this bill and I am going to vote for it, but it stinks." The remark made a deep impression upon me. I thought that if a man who had been a spearhead in the House in every fight for foreign aid and who was one of the principal exponents of this measure felt that way about it, I was not going to swallow it. I decided I would vote against the bill and thus force the committee to bring in a better one—one which contained less expensive installations to tempt the Communists and more food and medicine, tools and weapons that the South Koreans needed so badly.

I believed then, and I still do, that mine was the right stance, but here is what happened. The bill was defeated by one vote. Two or three weeks later a more acceptable bill was brought in and we passed it. In the meantime, however, the storm broke in Korea, and every man who voted against the original bill for Korean aid became a target. Not only that, every man who voted against it was held personally responsible for its defeat, because it had lost by but a single vote. This was thrown in my face in at least two campaigns thereafter. *I* was the villain who was responsible.

If I have given the impression that congressmen go about the House in fear and trembling, with knees knocking, afraid that they will guess wrong in casting an important vote, I want to correct that impression. There is a period in a young congressman's life, after he has first burned his fingers by a vote such as I have described, when he gets "gun shy" and sensitive; but after two or three campaigns for re-election the average congressman recovers, in large measure, from that sense of fear. This is partly because he is surer of himself and from experience has acquired a background of facts and information on the main problems that recur in every session. But it is mainly because of the practical lesson he has learned, that one can never foresee which of the votes he has cast will be the subject of attack when he goes home to the electorate. He remembers how he lay awake at night worrying about, and passed through an agony of indecision before casting a vote on, some national or international policy bound to have repercussions for years to come, and then, when he returned home for his next election campaign, he heard nothing whatsoever about that world-shattering matter, but was hounded from town to town because of his vote on some bill of such minor importance that at first he could not remember how he voted on it.

In one congressional session I voted against the "Rankin Bonus Bill," which provided billions of dollars for immediate cash handouts to all veterans. The bill was defeated by one vote, and I expected I would have to fight for my political life because of it. On the contrary, I hardly ever heard of it again, and when it was mentioned, I found that most of the veterans in my district regarded it as an unwarranted raid on the treasury and commended me for my vote. However, in the same campaign I caught "Hail Columbia" because of a position I had taken in a letter I had written regarding a bill to prohibit the use of live dogs for scientific experiments in the District of Columbia. That bill had never come out of committee, never been voted on in the House, and I could not, indeed, even recall writing the letter in question.

Such experiences cause the seasoned member of Congress to become something of a fatalist. He knows the public fancy is uncertain, that popular concern springs up in strange and unexpected places, and that people often get excited about the little things rather than the big ones. Therefore, he knows there is no possible way of foreseeing which of his votes will come back to haunt him, so he might as well banish fear and meet each issue, regardless of how hotly it is debated or how many letters he receives upon it, calmly and without loss of sleep.

Oftentimes more important than how one votes is how many votes one misses. A representative's constituents will tolerate occasional, necessary absences. However, quite rightly, they will not forgive his failure to answer to a high percentage of roll-call votes. Members strive not to be away from Capitol Hill when the House is in session; but there are necessary exceptions. For example, one morning I broke the crown off a front tooth and immediately started beseeching my dentist for an emergency appointment. In Washington, as elsewhere, dentists are busy men. It is almost easier to get a quick appointment with the president. Accordingly, when my dentist said he would at once try to squeeze me in between appointments, I rushed frantically downtown for my temporary repairs. I was, however, hardly in the chair when my office telephoned that a roll call was starting in the House. I left the amazed (and disgusted) dentist flat and tore breathlessly back to the Capitol. It happened that I had not missed a roll call for months, and I did not want to miss this one. I bribed the taxi driver to hurry, and we arrived just under the wire, although every red light in town had seemed to be against us. And on what do you suppose I found myself voting? Was it some critical decision involving the fate of the nation? No, indeed! The question was, "Shall we increase the subsidy on peanuts?" I voted "No." I was against the program—and, besides, it was on peanuts that I had broken my tooth.

CHAPTER

III

Early Days in the Senate

> The U.S. Senate may not be the most refined and de-
> liberative body in existence but they got the most
> unique rules. Any member can call anybody in the
> world anything he can think of and they can't answer
> him, sue him, or fight him. Our constitution protects
> aliens, drunks and U.S. Senators. There ought to be
> one day (just one) when there is open season on
> senators.
>
> —*Will Rogers*

IT IS AN undeniable fact that for anyone who has been exposed in
youth, as I was, to the clash of personalities, the strife, and the turbu-
lence that go on endlessly in the Senate, there is quite apt to exist a
subconscious yearning to return. This must be true of almost all the
young people who have had occasion to serve on the staffs of committees or of senators. I know this to be so because of the number of colleagues with whom I served in the Senate who years before had been
staffers, although they were of more recent vintage than I—Senators
Alan Bible of Nevada, Russell Long of Louisiana, Joseph O'Mahoney
and Gale McGee of Wyoming, Dennis Chavez of New Mexico, and
Robert Kennedy of New York. And from my early days working on
the Hill, I recall that Senators Albert B. Cummins of Iowa and Robert
M. La Follette Jr. of Wisconsin had been staff members before they
themselves came to the Senate. Doubtless a search of the records
would identify many others who as young men were exposed to the
same "bug" and eventually returned. Of course, for everyone who re-

turned, there are many more who did not, some because they became immersed in other activities and lost the urge, others because they failed in their attempts to be elected. In most cases, those who have tried unsuccessfully have, it should be acknowledged, not failed for lack of ability or capacity. There is no denying that pure luck is a big factor in political life. Frequently, an even more decisive factor is timing—striking when the iron is hot.

In fact, just how does one get to be a U.S. senator? During my years as a member of Congress, young people, mostly college students, would ask me quite seriously, "How does one go about getting to Congress?" They would even seek advice on what courses they should take in college. Students rarely ask these questions nowadays. They are much more sophisticated. Colleges are placing greater emphasis on political science and government. Furthermore, hundreds of students have served "internships" in Washington.

During the first year of my retirement, I was given the opportunity of holding seminars with the students at Dartmouth College. It was a most interesting and illuminating experience, and I was amazed to find how much the students knew about the workings of both the Senate and House. It was disconcerting to find that in some respects their general knowledge exceeded mine—perhaps because a senator or a congressman is so immersed in those issues and problems handled by the committees on which he serves that he sees the trees rather than the forest, and has only a limited opportunity to take a really broad view or to study all the manifold activities of the entire Congress. However that may be, it was encouraging to find that the students who had served in the offices of senators and congressmen were fully aware that, by and large, members work hard and put in long hours, and that the drones do not stay there long. In other words, these student observers do not wholly share the general public's current contempt for and distrust of politicians.

Present-day students are interested in how to enter Congress, but their questions tend to be on what vocational activity provides the best springboard to get into politics. Should it be by way of the law? Or by entering the newspaper or television field? Or by starting with an advertising or public relations firm? Also, should one, they inquire, begin by running for minor offices, and perhaps serve in the state legislature, when one's real ambition is to reach, eventually, the Senate?

Of course, there is no obvious road to the Senate—no magic formula for getting there. In my own case, as I have already noted, I was a country lawyer and "moved up through the chairs": county prosecutor, municipal judge, floor leader and then speaker of the state legislature, and a member of the national House of Representatives for eight years, before finally going to the Senate. It is true that down through the years lawyers have gravitated toward public office, in both state and nation. Not long ago a canvass of the Congress showed that more than half the entire membership had been practicing lawyers or at least members of the bar. Apparently, this has been more or less the case throughout our history. Back in 1820, for instance, Thomas Jefferson in his autobiography, commenting on an earlier and smaller Congress, said:

> If the present Congress err in too much talking, how can it be other-
> wise, in a body to which the people send 150 lawyers, whose trade
> is to question everything, yield nothing, and talk by the hour?

(Of course, Jefferson, a lawyer himself, said a few words during his career.)

There were others in Jefferson's time, or even earlier, who apparently did not hold the legal profession in high esteem. When I cleared out the attic of my family home in Warren, New Hampshire, after my mother's death, I unearthed an old, tattered volume entitled *The Grafton County Gazetteer*, published, I believe, sometime in the 1840s. It consisted largely of biographical sketches of prominent inhabitants of that period, and it also contained some historical data of the past. Included was a report, in the nature of a census, made shortly before the Revolution, when most of the settled region, containing what are now Grafton, Sullivan, and Cheshire counties, was loosely called a "county." The author of the report was an undergraduate at Dartmouth, apparently with a religious bent of mind, and I was amused at the summarization in his concluding paragraph:

We have a county of over three thousand square miles, a population of six thousand five hundred and forty-nine souls, of which ninety are students at Dartmouth College and twenty are slaves. We have twenty-five incorporated towns all in a thriving condition, including fourteen grist mills, five saddler shops, seven millwrights, eight physicians, seventeen clergymen and not a single lawyer. For this happy state of affairs we take no credit unto ourselves, but render all the glory to God.

The law is by no means the only pathway to the Senate today. (Indeed, my guess would be that there is a smaller percentage of lawyers in that body now than ever before.) Actually, there are a thousand routes by which men find their way into Congress. My curiosity on this matter led me to conduct something of a canvass among my colleagues. I found that in most cases these individuals had never planned or expected to go to the Senate or the House. By the same token, most of the college boys who have that ambition in mind will probably end up in other fields of activity, while some of their classmates who have not the slightest interest in politics or public life will one day be making our laws.

What brings men to Congress depends oftentimes on the type of state or community in which they reside or on some social or political upheaval that has taken place. I had one friend in the House who came from a "machine" state. After he finished engineering school and service in World War I, he found himself married and up against the practical necessity of getting a job. He went to work in the engineering department of the highway commission of his state. To obtain that position, he had to be recommended by the local "leader" or "boss." In return for the job, he became a ward or precinct worker for the organization. Gradually, he was elevated from one position to another in the party hierarchy, until one day the powers that be informed him they were sending him to Congress. It is not to be inferred from this story that my colleague was in any sense the kind of low-brow thug many people picture when they think of a member of a political machine. Actually, he was a fine character, an active church worker, and a most earnest and conscientious congressman. The point is that the way in which he came to Congress was the result of his environment, and the conditions that prevailed in his state. Many members, particularly those from metropolitan areas, reach Congress the same way.

Another congressional colleague of mine had been a high school history teacher. His interest in politics had been purely academic, and nothing was further from his mind than seeking public office; however, he interested himself in a reform movement in his city, participated in several campaigns, and finally was elected mayor. He liked the taste of public life thus experienced, and after serving several terms as mayor, he ran for Congress and was elected.

(Parenthetically, may I add that it was interesting to note the effect of Congress upon these two friends. After a few years in the House, the history teacher was still a reformer, but was much more practical, restrained, and realistic in his approach. The product of the "machine" was still a machine politician, but he had acquired a national and international viewpoint and, according to my observation, had grown more idealistic with the years. Such is the tempering influence of life on Capitol Hill.)

It is really a case of "you take the high road and I'll take the low road, and I'll get to Congress afore ye," because although about half the Congress have been lawyers, many of them country lawyers like myself, and a large percentage have come up through state legislatures as I did, there are almost an equal number who have come from walks of life that are a far cry from politics. In both the House and the Senate I served with colleagues who had been professors, school superintendents, labor leaders, agricultural county agents, country editors, newscasters, social workers, ranchers, and businessmen. Anyone familiar with the diverse tasks and problems of a national legislator knows that no academic course in government that was ever taught and no particular single vocation can equip a person for the Senate, much less get him there. His training must be the practical lessons of everyday life, whether they be learned in the countinghouse or the courtroom. The truly fundamental requisite qualities for becoming and remaining a senator are a knowledge of human nature, a genuine liking for people, so that one is never bored by them or weary of being with them, and a plentiful supply of common sense.

There have been two significant changes in the routes from which the Senate draws its membership that have developed in the last twenty years. The first one I have just noted—that the legal profession has lost the near monopoly it enjoyed in yesteryears, so that the background of the present-day senator includes a broad diversity of vocations. The second is a particularly interesting—and in some ways quite surprising—change.

Ever since the federal Constitution was adopted and the U.S. Senate came into being, a large number, probably a majority, of its members have previously been governors of their respective states. In fact, attaining the governorship was formerly almost a requisite to becoming a senator. This was generally true throughout the country and almost universally true in the southern states. On the day of the state funeral of my senior colleague, Senator Styles Bridges, I remember taking Senator Russell of Georgia, who for years had been the leader of the Senate's southern bloc, through our state capitol in Concord. He looked with interest at the portraits of former governors of New Hampshire and then suddenly asked me, "What years were you governor?" I replied that I had never been governor, that I came to the Senate by way of the national House of Representatives. He made no comment, but I noted his look of surprise. Of course, there are a number of members of the present Senate who have been governors, but if you go over the whole roster, you will find that in the last twenty years, a larger number have been promoted to the Senate from the House of Representatives.

In many respects membership in the House is better preparation for service in the Senate than the governorship of a state. Although the rules and procedures in the House differ from those of the Senate, both bodies face the same national and international issues and problems, many of which constantly recur through the years. Both bodies are divided into similar committees, which work together jointly in the final stages of bills. Rules of seniority, although not identical, and which have been subject to many recent changes, prevail in some form in both bodies. For these and other reasons, senators who have served an apprenticeship in the House are able to adjust themselves to the ways of the Senate more quickly and more easily than those who come to it by other routes.

It is interesting to note that former House members seem to pass through their periods as "freshmen" senators with much more contentment and peace of mind than do former governors. My initial realization of this fact came to me when I first became really acquainted with Senator Edmund Muskie of Maine. The warm personal friendship we have enjoyed, in spite of political differences, began when we found ourselves seated together on a plane from Washington to Boston, exchanging confidences regarding both our earlier years, spent in neighboring states, and our reactions since coming to the Senate. He told me how frustrated and unhappy he had been during his first term in the Senate. "A governor," said Ed, "has for a term of years become accustomed to being the 'top dog' in his state. He plans programs and projects and, if he maintains a reasonable rapport with his legislature, gets them enacted into law and puts them into practice. In a large measure, he fixes the policy and exercises control over every division, department, and bureau of his state, because he appoints their heads and recommends their budget allowances to the legislature."

Senator Muskie then told me of the thrill that comes to a retiring governor when he goes to Washington as a member of perhaps the most powerful and exclusive legislative body in the world, the U.S. Senate—and of the disillusionment that comes to a governor after he is sworn in as a freshman member of that body. Inflexible rules of seniority start him at the very bottom of the ladder. He is assigned one of the least desirable offices. He occupies a back seat in the Senate. He does not rate membership on any of the blue-ribbon committees, and he sits at the bottom of the committees to which he is appointed. In every committee hearing he has to wait, before even asking a question, until the chairman and all the senior members have interrogated witnesses. He spends his time rushing to the Senate in response to roll calls and responding to letters from complaining constituents, most of whom demand that he pass legislation or perform other miracles that, at that point at least, are far beyond his power to achieve. Ed said it was at least four years before he felt he was anything more than a glorified errand boy, and that during those four years he resolved again and again that he would never seek another term. Of course, all that changed. The senator from Maine is now one of the leaders of his party, and he has been a serious contender for the presidency.

(Incidentally, I know of another governor who, because he was a member of the party in control of the Senate, was entitled to the chairmanship of a subcommittee. After administering the affairs of one of the larger states in the Union, he found himself chairing, of all things, the subcommittee that runs the Senate restaurant. Most of his time thereafter was occupied in listening to complaints about food and mediating squabbles between waiters. He was so disgusted he actually did refuse to run for a second term.)

I had moved from the House to the Senate three or four years before Ed Muskie became a senator, and I had been a member for some eight years when this conversation took place, but it was a revelation to me. I had never really had occasion, previously, to consider the frustrations of former governors in comparison with those of former House members.

It takes many long years for a member of the House to attain a position of influence, to become chairman of a committee or the top-ranking minority member. During those years most House members, consciously or subconsciously, have their eyes longingly on the Senate. Many of them fall by the wayside as a result of yielding to the temptation to run against a sitting senator, getting beaten, and finding themselves out of Congress altogether. Having observed the gnawing ambition of some of my colleagues and the disasters that followed, I resolved to enjoy my work and associations in the House and not to keep myself in a dither by looking for an opportunity to run for the Senate. If a real opportunity came, fine. If it did not, I would stay in the House and wait for the day when my seniority enabled me to play a really significant role in that body. It is one of life's contradictions that not long after I had achieved that tranquility of mind, Charles W. Tobey, the junior senator from New Hampshire, died. I ran and was elected to the vacant Senate seat, thus terminating my House service after eight years.

It is a sure bet that anyone who has ever served in the U.S. Senate, no matter how long that service may have been, will never forget his first days there. I have already laid some emphasis on the fact that service in the House is a good prepartion for service in the Senate. Now, using parliamentary language, I am compelled to amend that statement. It is true that the House deals with the same problems and issues as does the Senate, that it has a similar committee structure, and that in many matters concerning legislation a member of the House moving over to the Senate can, in a sense, take up pretty much where he left off. But when you get away from these basics, the former House member finds himself entering a new and different world. To be sure, ancient customs and traditions of the Senate which were jealously guarded and maintained for 150 years have been considerably modified during the last decade. But enough of them remain so that they are an eye opener for a newcomer, even though he may have had previous service in the House.

One of the first matters that a new member faces is the assignment of an office. This is the same in both the Senate and the House: senior members select vacant offices in order of their seniority, and the newcomers get the leftovers. The next subject of interest is committee appointments. In this, as in many other aspects of life in the Senate, seniority is an important factor. However, there have been so many controversies about the system of seniority and so many modifications, particularly in the last ten years of my service, that I will not try to cover it here, but will devote a later chapter to the subject.

Next comes the assignment of seats in the Senate. Here seniority still reigns supreme and, again, the newcomer takes what is left. But being assigned a desk and a seat is, of course, a new experience for former House members. In the House, with its 435 members, there are no desks and there is no assignment of seats. Members sit wherever they choose, except that Republicans occupy the right side of the House and Democrats the left, and the seats behind the tables at the front of the chamber, on each side of the aisle, are reserved for party leaders and for the managers of whatever bill happens to be under consideration at any given time. (Throughout my service in the House and since, all the Republican congressmen from Pennsylvania have by custom sat together at the rear of the Republican side, next to the center aisle. Knowing this, other members, as a matter of courtesy, refrain from taking those seats. I do not know of any other state delegation that insists on sitting together. It would seem to reflect a little clannishness on the part of the Pennsylvanians, and it has always reminded me of a remark made by the president of Haverford College, "Quakers believe in the fatherhood of God, the brotherhood of man, and the neighborhood of Philadelphia.")

For more than a hundred years senators invariably wore formal morning clothes when appearing on the floor of the Senate. As late as fifty years ago, when I was a staffer, most of the Senate appeared in this formal garb on special occasions, such as the inauguration of a president, the delivery of the president's annual message on the State of the Union, the annual reading of Washington's Farewell Address on his birthday, or when the Senate was visited by a foreign dignitary. When I entered the Senate a quarter-century ago, cutaway coats and striped trousers had entirely disappeared (perhaps the senators sold them secondhand to the State Department; diplomats still wear them). Members were, however, expected to wear conservative business suits during sessions of the Senate, and I had been serving about ten years when Dick Neuberger of Oregon, who was an able senator but somewhat of a maverick, defied custom and appeared on the floor in a sport coat and slacks. I recall how horrified some of the seniors were. But the wearing of such informal attire is now pretty well established, except on special occasions. Indeed, on some days the Senate is spotted with bright colors, checks, and plaids—somewhat to the disgust of the old-timers. (Once, when I had been confined to all-day hearings before the Appropriations Committee, I went on the floor of the Senate, to answer a roll call, wearing a deep-red sport jacket. My good friend Milton Young of North Dakota, who has been in the Senate well over thirty years and is the senior ranking Republican, looked at me sharply and asked, "Where are the hounds?")

There being no Senate rule on the matter of proper dress, such criticism as has manifested itself has been privately expressed and has not been the subject of open discussion within the Senate. As far as I know, the matter has been formally raised but once on the floor, and I am the guilty one who brought it up. A free-lance writer, Vera Glaser, wrote an article entitled "The 10 Best and Worst Dressed U.S. Senators." The article, which was later published in Washington, first came to my attention in a Boston newspaper. It was too good to keep to myself, so on an afternoon when only minor concerns were before us, I arose on a point of personal privilege and brought it to the attention of the Senate. I could appropriately do so, because I was numbered among the ten worst-dressed senators—indeed, I was treated perhaps the most harshly of all, because the good lady described me as looking like "an over-sized gunny sack." I insisted that I was not unduly upset, but I suggested to my fellow senators that it was a little discouraging to put on a clean shirt and a fairly recently pressed dark suit on days when the Senate was in session and then be referred to in such terms.

With some delight, I quoted Miss Glaser's comments on other senators. Interestingly, more and more senators came to the floor when word of what was being discussed got about. The group of the "best-dressed" was headed by Republican John Tower of Texas, described as "dapper" and a former college professor who "wears detachable collars and has his suits tailored in London." By contrast, socially prominent Democrat Claiborne Pell topped the frump list: "He once wore the same seersucker suit five days running." Following Tower in the "peacock parade" were Connecticut's Abe Ribicoff and South Dakota's George McGovern ("who went 'Ivy League' in the 1972 campaign"). "Flashiest and handsomest" on the list were Oregon's Mark Hatfield and Massachusetts's Edward Brooke.

Two senators described but not placed on either list because they were too "wild" of garb were Wyoming's Gale McGee and Nebraska's Carl Curtis. McGee was described as wearing a "lurid orange shirt, wide-lapelled, brown-striped suit, and electric tie." Curtis, the article said, "was known as the dour type until a year ago, when he married for the second time. . . . Wreathed in smiles these days, Curtis has blossomed out in mod finery. He drapes his stocky form in geometric double-knits, pointed yokes, back pleats, flared pants and ascot ties." ("Such trends," the article said, "are revolutionary for the Senate, which not too long ago had the sergeant-at-arms evict an aide in a loud plaid suit.")

Pell appeared and defended himself, recalling advice given him by a senior senator: "There are two kinds of people around here, workhorses and show horses." "I am not a show horse," Pell said. Tower, arriving on the floor, said the article "has probably done me irreparable political damage in my state, because people in Texas do not necessarily cotton to people who patronize London tailors."

The discussion was accompanied by considerable laughter and light-hearted humor, and I brought it to a close by inserting the entire article in the record and saying that I had not raised the subject in anger, but because it might be helpful if we could "see ourselves as others see us." Though the whole matter was treated in the spirit of mirth, I am not sure that Miss Glaser's observations were entirely wasted, for it seemed to me that afterward senators were perhaps a little more careful in their mode of dress on days that the Senate was in session.

There are formalities other than dress that have been traditional in the Senate, and which, although not entirely abolished, have also been somewhat relaxed. I recall in my early days in the Senate, if one senator referred to another by name, he was instantly called to order by the chair, because it was the rule—and still is—that any reference to other senators be in the form of "the senator from . . ." (naming of the state). Even that rule is not now rigidly enforced, save when some senior senator, who is a traditionalist, happens to be presiding. Of course, the reason for the rule is the fact that senators represent states, whereas members of the House represent people.

The sovereignty in this nation rests in the states, except insofar as they have surrendered portions of their sovereignty to the federal government. During part of our history it was considered by many that a state, having joined the Union, had a perfect right to secede from it. Senators were therefore treated almost as ambassadors from the states they represented. Of course, this concept was settled forever on the battlefields of the Civil War, but the form of address still remains a tradition and a rule of the Senate.

It is somewhat amusing to note that one can usually tell from the degree of formality with which one senator refers to another what the nature of their personal relations may be. If the reference is made casually as "Senator Jones," they are probably close friends. If someone refers to a colleague simply as "the senator from Michigan," one may infer that they have a cordial relationship. If a senator refers to another as "the distinguished senator from Indiana," one may assume he does not particularly like him. And if he refers to him as "the very able and distinguished senator from California," it usually indicates he hates his guts.

Of course, there are other distinctions between procedure in the House and Senate, most of them too trivial to warrant describing here. There is one difference, however, which although really of minor importance has been particularly irritating to former House members who arrive in the Senate. Throughout the years, a quorum call in the House has been taken seriously. It has counted on a member's record as if it were a vote. The reason was that it required at least forty-five minutes to call the roll in the House—accordingly, something rarely resorted to without cause. Perhaps the recent installation of an electrical voting system has speeded up the process, so that the House may now be less sparing in resorting to roll calls, but I doubt it. To be sure, members can register their vote instantly when they reach the floor, but time still must be given for hundreds of individuals to come from their offices.

Through the years, House members have dropped everything to get to the floor for quorum calls, and once a quorum call is started, it always goes through to the end. The Senate is quite different.

Whenever a little time is needed to enable the managers of a bill to negotiate, or to permit a senator to reach the floor, someone suggests the absence of a quorum; the bells ring and the clerk starts calling the roll. As soon as the absent senator arrives or the matter is adjusted, the quorum call is withdrawn. As an ex-member of the House, I did not at the outset understand this, and I remember that during my first week or two in the Senate, I nearly ran my legs off, dashing from my office to the floor to answer quorum calls, only to find when I arrived that the call had been withdrawn and there was no reason for my presence. This exasperation has been experienced by almost all House members entering the Senate—until some kindly colleague explains to them that unless a third bell rings, indicating a "live" quorum, there is no real need to dash to the floor.

On this point, I have a favorite story about the senator who was hosting several guests in his Capitol office, watching a World Series baseball game on television while the Senate was in session. The bells rang twice. One of his guests kept looking at the senator, thinking he would immediately start for the floor. Finally, noting that his guest was regarding him expectantly, the senator asked, "What's the matter with you?" "I thought I heard a quorum call," replied his guest. "No doubt you did," said the senator brusquely, "this is their mating season."

There are many signal bells that sound in the Senate, its cloak-rooms, restaurants, committee rooms, and in senators' offices. They can be confusing to both visitors and newcomers, and sometimes even to seasoned members. There is one long ring at the hour of convening. One short bell signifies a roll-call vote. Two is for a regular quorum call. Three, as I have indicated, is for a live quorum. Four is for adjournment or recess. Five indicates there are only five minutes remaining on a yea and nay vote, and six indicates the close of the morning business.

Still speaking of bells, there was a supposedly true incident which has long been a subject of much mirth in the Senate. A senator was entertaining an elderly lady constituent. Other duties made it impossible for him to conduct her personally to the Senate gallery, so he sent a young page with her to identify senators and to explain what was taking place. Unfortunately, the lad had been a page only a short time and he was not much better informed than the old lady herself. It was a busy session, and bells were constantly ringing for quorum calls and roll calls. "Why," queried the lady, "do these bells ring so constantly and so stridently?" The boy did not have the answer, but after a moment's hesitation, he said, "I'm not quite sure, but I think maybe one of them has escaped."

Until very recently, there has been a traditional ceremony in which new senators have gone through what was called the "snuff" initiation. It has been many years since any senators took snuff, but the rather ornate snuff box attached to the wall near the presiding officer has been maintained and is periodically freshly filled by Senate attendants. On a day selected during the first two weeks of every session of Congress, the whole Senate would look on, with broad grins, while the new members were escorted to this box and invited to take snuff, as Webster and Clay used to do. I had heard that in the past some budding statesmen had nearly strangled in the course of this ceremony, so when it came my turn, I decided that in taking snuff I definitely would be a "moderate." The late Senator Flanders of Vermont loved to conduct the freshmen through the ceremony. Since his departure, however, I cannot recall witnessing this tradition.

Some of the historical sidelights of the Senate have always fascinated me. One is the story of the Senate desks, as gleaned from Emery Frazier, who was for many years chief clerk of the Senate and who made researching their history his hobby. In 1819 when the first steamship was breasting the Atlantic, and Maine and Alabama were knocking at the door for statehood, the Senate resumed sessions in the old chamber which had been burned by the British five years before. At that time new desks, believed to be about forty-eight in number, were built and installed. In 1859, nearly 120 years ago, these were moved into the present chamber when the new and enlarged Capitol was completed. Thereafter, other desks were added as states were admitted to the Union. Of course, the last four were for new senators from Alaska and Hawaii, bringing the total number of desks to 100. Obviously, some of the original forty-eight, having become worn and battered, were from time to time discarded and replaced. A few that had been used by historic senators were rescued and restored. The oldest ones can be distinguished from the modern desks because they are slightly smaller, have just one drawer, and their lids cannot be lifted for additional space.

At the feet of each desk are attached perforated metal shields called "diffusers," formerly used for ventilation. Many objected when the present chamber was built, because it had no outside windows. Claustrophobic senators insisted they would suffocate, so a system was devised for ventilation through the floor. Floor ventilators would have been too tempting for tobacco chewers, hence the hollow legs with perforated shields. This system has, with modern air conditioning, long since been abandoned—and so has the tobacco chewing (although it is rumored that Senator Talmadge of Georgia still indulges occasionally).

The desks have been moved back and forth from one side of the aisle to the other, as party majorities have ebbed and flowed. The "center" aisle has not always actually been in the center, as it is today. For instance, in the early days of FDR, it was well over to the right, leaving room for only sixteen Republican desks.

The history of some of the Senate desks is known. When I came to the Senate, Styles Bridges, New Hampshire's senior senator, had Daniel Webster's old desk. With the assistance of Emery Frazier he had discovered it in a basement room of the Capitol and had it restored. (It had "DW" carved with a knife on the bottom of the drawer.) When Senator Bridges died in 1961 and I became senior senator, I lost no time in claiming the Webster desk. (There had been some whispers to the effect that, after all, Daniel Webster represented Massachusetts in the Senate, not New Hampshire, and why shouldn't his desk go, therefore, to a Massachusetts senator. But I had no difficulty in securing the desk. Senator Leverett Saltonstall, one of the finest gentlemen who ever served in the Senate, made no objection, and I outranked his junior colleague. True, Daniel Webster as a senator did represent Massachusetts, but he was born in New Hampshire, was educated at Exeter and Dartmouth, and practiced law in and went to Congress from Portsmouth. His name has long been linked with New Hampshire tradition.) The desk had to be moved, because my seniority was not then sufficient for me to inherit Senator Bridges' position on the floor, but a few years later my added seniority entitled me to the aisle seat in the second row, just back of the minority leadership, so the Daniel Webster desk returned to its place.

Just before retiring from the Senate at the end of 1974, I introduced a Senate resolution that the Webster desk should always remain with the senior Senator from New Hampshire. (I confess that I had my resolution brought up for immediate consideration one afternoon when both Massachusetts senators were out of town. I easily secured its adoption. But Senator Saltonstall had in the meantime retired, anyway, and neither of the Bay State senators then serving had enough seniority to stop me.) Naturally, I was a little sorry to know that on my retirement the Webster desk would go across the aisle to the Democratic side. Yet, at the same time, I was glad to have it go to Senator Tom McIntyre, my warm personal friend. Moreover, political fortunes change, and unless the Republican party disintegrates, as some prophets of gloom have been predicting, the desk may at some future time return to our side, where Daniel Webster himself sat as a member of the Whig party. At any rate, the desk will be used by New Hampshire senators henceforth unless my resolution should be repealed, which is unlikely.

There are other historic desks in the chamber. Senator John Stennis of Mississippi sits at the one used before the Civil War by Jefferson Davis. A block of mahogany plugs the hole in its side where Union soldiers, returning from the war, plunged their bayonets as a last stab at "Jeff Davis." It has recently been established that Senator Russell Long of Louisiana is using the Calhoun desk.

The vice president's desk, removed when the Senate chamber

was redecorated in the late 1940s or early 1950s, was, by resolution, presented to Senator Alben Barkley, to be his for life and then to be placed in the Kentucky state capitol. This action was taken because the first vice president to use it was a Kentuckian, John C. Breckinridge, and the last was Barkley himself, also a Kentuckian.

The history of the back-row desk that I had as a freshman senator is not known, although one day I discovered in the bottom of the drawer names of senators, scrawled in pencil and almost illegible, as well as some initials, carved with a knife—mute evidence of the human desire to perpetuate one's name, whether one is a U.S. senator or just a schoolboy hacking away at his desk with a jackknife. I was a bit tempted to carve my own initials there, but I remembered that the last time I tried desk carving, a teacher had blistered my backside with a strap. (Of course, that was before educators decided that corporal punishment crushes the spirit and warps the personality.)

As in retirement I write these impressions and memories, I naturally think with nostalgia of my years in both the House and the Senate, and of the men and women with whom I served, most of them no longer living. All those years of service never dulled the thrill that came to me with the opening of each session of Congress. As I flew into Washington a familiar scene unfolded: the Capitol, the Library of Congress, the stately buildings down Constitution Avenue, the huge Pentagon across the river—the government seat of a mighty nation. Looking down on the sharp shaft of Washington's Monument, one could almost hear his voice saying, "Government . . . is force! Like fire it is a dangerous servant and a fearful master; never for a moment should it be left to irresponsible action."

I remember still that, following custom, early in the morning of the day that the Eighty-fourth Congress convened—the first Congress after I had taken my oath as a senator—most of the top officials of the government attended a service of intercession at a local church (this time the National Presbyterian, where President Eisenhower worshiped). It was an inspiring thing to sit with the members of the House and Senate, the cabinet, the generals and admirals of our armed forces; to kneel, with the president himself only a few feet away; and to listen to the time-honored litany:

Almighty God . . . uphold by thy Might the President of these United States. Preserve him in health of body, serenity of soul and soundness of judgment. Grant him . . . a constant and confident faith in Thee. . . .

CHAPTER

IV

The Impact of the Seventeenth Amendment
upon Congress

Experience should teach us to be most on our guard to
protect liberty when the government's purposes are be-
neficent.

—*Louis Brandeis*

ALMOST everyone has either forgotten or never fully realized the impact on Congress of one of the most dynamic presidents in the history of the United States. Theodore Roosevelt in one fell swoop
utterly changed the character of both houses of Congress. It was he
who pushed through the Seventeenth Amendment of the Constitution, providing that U.S. senators be chosen by popular vote instead
of by their state legislatures. At first blush, any person who believes
in bringing our government closer to the people would say that this
was a good change to make, and perhaps it was. But good or bad, it
eventually created a new heaven and new earth, as far as the American Congress was concerned.

One cannot follow the proceedings of the convention that wrote
the Constitution or analyze the individual views of those who framed
it, as reflected in the "Federalist Papers," without sensing the constant and sometimes bitter strife between those who wanted to get
as far away from the British monarchy as possible, by creating an
absolute democracy, and those who believed in a representative form
of government responsive, but not too immediately responsive, to the
demands of the populace. Neither side prevailed; the struggle re-

sulted in a compromise. A national House of Representatives was created whose members would be elected every two years by the people, thus reflecting the prevailing mood of the voters at any particular time, even though that mood might prove to be a temporary wave of sentiment. As a counterbalance, members of the Senate were to be elected by the legislatures of the respective states, each for a term of six years, with selection so staggered that only one-third would be chosen at any biennial election. The theory was that the Senate would eventually reflect those desires of the people which were fixed and firm, but would not be immediately responsive to every passing popular fancy.

There were those who were so fearful of this dual solution that they opposed the creation of two houses in our national legislature and favored a unicameral Congress, directly elected by the people. There is a tradition that Thomas Jefferson, upon his return from France, protested to President Washington against the establishment of two houses. The incident occurred, it is said, at the breakfast table, and by way of response Washington asked, "Why did you pour coffee into your saucer?" "To cool it," replied Jefferson. "Even so," said Washington, "we pour legislation into the senatorial saucer to cool it."

The full impact of the change to a direct election of senators, which took effect early in this century, was not immediately discernible. Many of the powerful members of the Senate at that time had become so well known and so firmly entrenched that they continued to be elected by their people, as they had previously been elected by the legislatures. However, as time went on and these men passed from the scene, the real force of the Seventeenth Amendment began to be felt. It appeared that the new system had put the fear of God —or, rather, the fear of the people—into the Senate, and that both branches of the Congress would be forced to be, in fact, immediately responsive to popular demand at all times. Then, as the years passed, a strange and paradoxical development took place. It could not have been foreseen and probably still remains a mystery to many. The

Senate became the radical and impulsive body, while the House, in normal times at least, became the branch of more conservative restraint.

Why has this reversal taken place? The answer is not hard to find, if one takes a look at political geography. Consider the major states of the Union, which dominate the House of Representatives. In these states, one finds large metropolitan areas and rural areas. Each of these states includes a considerable number of congressional districts. Urban districts are usually overwhelmingly Democratic; they are liberal, and largely dominated by organized labor. Rural districts tend to be Republican; they are conservative, and principally engaged in small business and agriculture. There are, of course, a certain proportion of borderline districts that swing back and forth. These are mostly suburban domains, composed of both city and country dwellers—and in some of these large universities are located, where the academic community has considerable impact. I think it is safe to say, however, that a substantial majority of the members of the House of Representatives come from districts that are solidly or predominantly one way or the other. That means each of these congressmen is chosen because his political philosophy is in tune with that of the overwhelming majority of his constituents, and this makes his task comparatively simple. He votes his own convictions, which happily coincide with the convictions of those he represents. He does not, by and large, need to worry or fret about how he is going to vote, for both his convictions and his decisions come ready-made.

A senator's constituency, on the other hand, covering a whole state, includes all elements—urban and rural, labor and agriculture, liberal and conservative. Though he may not hope to satisfy all these groups, he is constantly striving not to alienate any of them unnecessarily. Thus, it is easy to see why the House of Representatives usually takes a more determined and definitive stance than does the Senate, whose members must constantly seek to compromise and appease all the varying elements within their home states. While it can be persuasively argued that the direct election of U.S. senators is consistent with government by the people, the inevitable result has been to give us a stronger House of Representatives and a weaker Senate.

The increase of the powers of the House, finding its real basis in the fact that under the rules of the larger body debate must be limited and the time of votes fixed (so there is always more action and less talk in the House), together with the far-reaching effects of the direct election of senators which I have just touched upon, has been receiving further impetus over two centuries by the constitutional provision that all tax bills must originate in that body. Furthermore, custom and precedent, as well as the fact that appropriation bills frequently suggest special taxes, have resulted in an almost ironclad rule that the House has the first crack at all spending bills. So, do not underrate your congressman. He is, to be sure, only one of 435, and he may not attract quite the publicity that a senator, being a member of a smaller and more select group, receives. Furthermore, unless he has been in Congress for many years and has become the chairman of a powerful committee, his crown and his scepter may not be visible. But a member of the House of Representatives is one of the midwives functioning at the birth of our fiscal policy—and Mr. and Mrs. John Q. Public would do well to remember it.

Before I confine my discussion largely to the Senate, where I spent most of my years, it might be appropriate to summarize briefly the powers exercised by both houses of Congress and to focus on how these powers have developed and expanded with the years. In the early days of the republic, the Congress confined itself almost exclusively to the authority explicitly conferred upon it by the Constitution: to control of the purse strings of the nation, with the sole power to levy taxes and provide money to operate the federal government, to declare war, to provide for the national defense, and to regulate interstate commerce. From a present-day standpoint, these are only the ABCs of the functions of Congress. As the nation has grown and modern life become more complex, constitutional provisions have been stretched—occasionally by amendment, but usually by judicial interpretation—to include a vast additional coverage.

The power to regulate commerce (the Founding Fathers could not have dreamed what a loophole that would prove to be) has been expanded by court decisions until the Congress, by legislation, can control almost completely the lives of all citizens. To this end, the Supreme Court has gone to almost ridiculous extremes. It has held that persons washing the windows of an office building in which even one office is occupied by a firm doing business in more than one state are engaged in interstate commerce, and their wages, hours, and conditions can be dictated from Washington. Similarly, a lighthouse, built and operated by a state or by a coastal county or city, shall come under federal control if the rays of its light are bright enough to be seen cross the borders of another state. And probably the wildest stretch of all was the court's decision that a roadside farmer selling to passing motorists sweet cider made from his own apples, or dainties made by his wife, is subject to federal control, even if such refreshment was consumed on his premises, because of the possibility that some portion of the beverage or food may remain in the stomachs of his customers after they have entered another state.

Recent examples of the exercise of such congressional powers are familiar to all: establishing and enforcing standards for the construction of automobiles; considering a national "no-fault" insurance law to supersede all state laws on that subject; restrictions of all kinds on energy, manufacturing, business, and even agriculture that in the opinion of Congress (or Ralph Nader) might pose a possible hazard to people or even to the environment. The Senate, through the Commerce Committee, on which I served, spent many days attempting to devise legislation governing athletic contests—revising the rules under which athletes might participate in the Olympic games, and even changing the rules of baseball, including contracts between owners and players.

Accordingly, one must not read the provisions of the Constitution as to the powers and duties of the Senate or the House and think that is the whole story. The powers and duties have been expanded a hundredfold—calling to mind Aesop's fable of the bullfrog that tried to blow itself up to match the size of an ox, until it finally exploded (which may well be the fate not only of the Congress, but the whole federal government, if it continues to magnify its powers and multiply its personnel).

The wholesale expansion of the powers and duties of Congress brought about equally sweeping changes in its organization and procedures to deal with this ever-growing authority. By far the most significant development, which is fast reaching the point where it poses a very real menace to the effectiveness of the American Congress and even a danger to the republic itself, is the phenomenal growth of congressional and committee staffs, and the delegation to them of functions that should be exercised only by senators and congressmen elected by the people.

When the Congress was in its infancy, members had no offices and no staffs, not even a secretary or stenographer. Sitting at their desks in the chamber, they wrote out in longhand such correspondence as they found necessary. Obviously, as both the nation and the Congress grew in size, this state of affairs could not continue. Senators and congressmen were provided some kind of an office, either within the Capitol itself or rented in the private buildings of the fast-growing capital city, and they were provided a secretary to assist them. Moreover, each committee came to have its clerk and sometimes an assistant clerk. It is noteworthy, though, that it was not until the early 1900s that Congress appropriated money for the erection of an office building for each body, in order to provide offices for members and their staffs and rooms for the increasing number of committees that could not be accommodated in the Capitol itself. These buildings were not ready for occupancy by the House and Senate until 1908 and 1909, respectively; and the old Senate Office Building was not actually completed until 1933.

When I went on Senator Moses' staff in 1925, each congressman had but one room. He sat at a desk and was partially hidden by a bookcase, on the other side of which were his secretary, a stenographer, and any people waiting to talk with him. The others in the room could not see the congressman, but they could hear him and see any person he might be interviewing at the time. There could be, under such conditions, no such thing as a private conversation. Senators in 1925 were, on the other hand, much more fortunate. Most of them had three rooms, although some of the juniors had only two.

Since the first decade of this century, the House has built two new office buildings, one of them the colossal Rayburn Building, which is so huge even members of the House get lost in it. The Senate has added one new office building and is about to build another. All this additional space has not been needed for the members themselves, who already had adequate offices and toilet facilities. (This is true even though five new states have been added to the Union since 1900.) No, this vast sprawling plant—including office buildings and space rented in numerous other buildings, as well as garages and parking lots—has been added because of other factors, which I shall take up in the next chapter.

But apropos of the office buildings, present and contemplated, I must relate briefly my experience of moving, after my first five years in the Senate, into the "new" Senate Office Building. I did this somewhat reluctantly, for there is more dignity and comfort in the old building, with its spacious offices and high ceilings, and I had a sentimental attachment to it, because there I had served many years ago with Senator Moses. However, both of my committees were quartered in the new building, and had I remained in the old building it would have meant tramping many miles and wasting many hours each year. The then-new building provides in some ways a fair example of the good and the bad, the necessary and the unnecessary, present in most government undertakings.

The new building was authorized before I came to the Senate, but undoubtedly I would have been for it—with limitations. The cost, although heavy for those days (twenty million dollars), was a drop in the bucket compared with the mighty structures of the huge departments downtown. But for a Senate that at that time was preaching (though obviously not practicing) economy, there are a few revealing and disturbing facts to be cited. The new building contains space for forty-two senators and their staffs, for twelve committees and their employees, for the busy Capitol telephone exchange, for a cafeteria and a basement garage—all essentials. However, it also includes a 500-seat auditorium, a gymnasium, and (imagine it!) a sun deck on the roof. Moreover, many of the committee rooms are larger and more pretentious than necessary. The building was in many respects poorly planned and wasteful of space. It reminds one of the schoolboy's essay on the camel: "The camel is an animal that looks like he was put together by a committee." The new office building was not only put together by a committee, but one that changed members constantly during construction.

The office conduits for telephones and electric wiring were so placed that Houdini himself would hardly have been able to squirm in and out from behind the desks. My own desk for years was so close to the wall that I was almost sitting on the window sill. In committee we were no longer able to sit around a table and chat informally with the witnesses. We were elevated on a circular dais behind a massive paneled bulwark. The barricade was so high we could not look at the witnesses without craning our necks. When pictures were taken at hearings, nothing was visible but the tops of our heads (a heartbreaking tragedy for a politician). The witness sat many feet from the committee, and the public considerably behind him. To cover these distances, the witness and each committee member was equipped with a microphone, but so defective was the sound system that we wailed like banshees and the noise drowned out all deliberations. (My own Committee on Commerce, which exercises dominion over television, radio, telephone, and all reproductions of the human voice throughout this broad land, had to adjourn its first hearing because it could not control its own squawks.) Despite expensive alterations, remodeling, and attempted corrections, this is still a problem. Besides the foregoing, the elevators were all automatic and when you pressed a button, you never knew which direction you were going or where you would wind up, if someone else beat you to the punch. I can still hear the senators, long accustomed, in the old building, to ringing three times and being sped to their destinations, fuming indignantly over the uncertainties of automation.

My senior colleague, New Hampshire's much-loved Styles Bridges, had been one of the original planners of this new building and was active on the committee that supervised its erection. I wrote one of my regular "Reports" to the people back home, describing in a humorous way some of the defects in the building. When I wrote it, I forgot completely that Senator Bridges was one of the principal planners. That was most unfortunate. One of the few incidents that ever disturbed our warm relationship was the fact that he resented my ridiculing the shortcomings in his pet project. He was even more irritated when I voted against appropriating more millions to install wall-to-wall carpeting over the fancy floors that soon proved to be hard on the feet of employees and, also, to excavate a new terminal under the Senate wing of the Capitol for the subways that connected both buildings with the Senate chamber. The appropriation passed, whereupon the committee in charge of the building, of which Bridges was the most influential member, instructed the superintendent of the Senate Office Buildings not to install carpets in the offices of those senators who had voted against the measure, unless they specifically asked for such in writing. I, in turn, became obstinate and refused to do this, much to the disgust of my staff. Mine remained the only office with bare floors, until increasing seniority caused me, later, to move to a more desirable location. This is an illustration of how U.S. senators are capable of behaving, on occasion, like little boys, but that petty quarrel with Senator Bridges was of short duration and did not breach our lifelong friendship.

Shortly after Bridges died in 1961, the Democratic leader of the Senate offered a resolution naming the original Senate Office Building in honor of Harry Truman. I immediately offered a similar resolution to name the new building after Styles Bridges, who had worked so long and hard to obtain it. At that time there was little sentiment within the Senate to attach anyone's name to either structure, so the

resolutions fell by the wayside. Years later, the old and the new buildings were by resolution named after Senator Russell of Georgia and
Senator Dirksen of Illinois, who had been leaders in the Senate and
who had died at about the same time. Although I had for years a warm
friendship with Everett Dirksen, I tried once again at that juncture to
attach Bridges's name to the new building. I failed. Styles had been
dead for several years, while the tears had not yet dried for Russell and
Dirksen. Senators, no matter how influential or powerful, are soon
forgotten when they disappear from the Senate floor.

Time has cured many of the new building's minor flaws and
"bugs," and the nation may take pride in this stately building of pure
white marble, within the walls of which its tenants have struggled
with many a momentous problem. Plaints concerning its original cost
seem now to be mere Yankee penny-pinching, and after all, one cannot put a price tag on statesmanship. I am reminded of the painter
employed to touch up the fresco work in a church. His itemized bill:
"Corrected the Ten Commandments–$6.20; Replumed and gilded
wings of the Guardian Angel–$15.75; Redecorated Noah's Ark–
$12.50; Mended shirt of Prodigal Son and cleaned his ears–$9.40.
Total: $43.85."

CHAPTER

V

Extension of Congressional Jurisdiction
and the Rise of Congressional Staffs

Beware of all enterprises that require new clothes.
—*Henry David Thoreau*

THE tremendous expansion of the plant operated by the Congress on
Capitol Hill—which has grown even faster than those of General
Motors—has had two principal causes: the ever-widening jurisdiction
of the Congress and the mushrooming of congressional staffs. It must
be said that the former cause of the two is something Congress could
not entirely control, but it must also be said that the Congress has
failed to make any diligent effort to control it.

Two World Wars, Korea, and Vietnam called millions of young
Americans into the armed forces and thousands of other Americans of
all ages into administrative posts concerned with the draft, the ration-
ing of food and fuel, the purchase of weapons and supplies, the production of new and needed materials, and the provision of hospital and
medical services. Most of these activities did not cease when hostilities
ended. Millions of veterans continued with us. Those with disabilities
had to be cared for, and every effort had to be made to find jobs for the
rest. Thus the emergencies of war caused the federal government to
place its paternal hand, in some measure, on the home, family, and
business of every individual citizen. And there it remains.

Millions of idealistic citizens sincerely believe that the federal
government can manage our lives and care for our needs better than
we can ourselves. These well-intentioned socialistic thinkers have be-

come so powerful that, with the aid of big labor, they dominate the
Congress, especially the Senate, and few aspirants to the presidency
have been able to win without their support. As a result, the federal
establishment has virtually taken over welfare, and it has greatly extended its support and control of health and education—leading to the
creation of the gigantic Department of Health, Education and Welfare, which towers over every other executive department, except perhaps Defense.

The federal government has embarked on a multitude of programs,
such as housing for the elderly, low-income housing, food stamps for
the needy, urban renewal for the slums, price supports for the farmers,
job training for the unemployed, Peace Corps and Vista for the youth.
The administration of all these programs—and countless others—by
federal bureaucrats has led inevitably to delays and inequalities, and
the untold thousands of individuals who have suffered because of
these inefficiencies have had no recourse but to write to their senator
or congressman. In this way, a vastly expanded activity has been created in every congressional or senatorial office. We call this "casework," and in recent years it alone has either doubled, tripled, or
quadrupled every congressional staff on Capitol Hill.

All these factors that I have enumerated, plus the growth in population of the nation, have been reflected in the size of staffs, particularly
in the Senate, where each member represents an entire state. Obviously, it would be impossible for senators to deal with their constantly
mounting new duties (some of them never even contemplated in
earlier days) without adequate assistance—but, as might be expected,
adequate always seems to be spelled with a capital A and two Ds.

Some years ago it became necessary to tie salary allowances for the
provision of senatorial staffs to the population of the states represented.
While I was a member the states were at first divided into three
groups, and only California and New York were in the top bracket.
This, however, soon brought protests from the large states in the mid-
dle group. So, a new and more complicated sliding scale was adopted.
Senators from California, with its twenty million people, and from
New York, with nearly nineteen million, had an allowance for staff

compensation of $709,650 each. States whose population fell between eleven and twelve million—namely, Illinois, Pennsylvania, and Texas —received slightly less. Ohio, having between ten and eleven million, was in a class by itself, as was Massachusetts, with a population of between five and six million. Senators from all states with less than two million people were allowed $370,215 for staff assistance (these include New Hampshire, Vermont, Delaware, Wyoming, and Maine).

There is no question but that members from large and populous states require substantial staffs. I have seen thirty and forty bulging mailbags being delivered in a single day to the offices of California, New York, and Illinois senators. Certainly, these senators would require at least thirty to forty people to handle that amount of mail. However, each time the senators from large states have asked for and received increased staff allowances, those from smaller states have insisted on *some* increase also. This has occurred because there is considerable sensitivity among members of the Senate, and for reasons that I never could quite fathom, senators from small states have felt that their responsibilities were being belittled if they did not receive at least a token increase concurrently. I never joined in the periodic protests of those from the smaller states. It always seemed obvious to me that a senator from New Hampshire did not need and could not wisely use up an allowance of $370,000. Except when some particular emergency necessitated my taking on temporary or part-time employees on a supplementary basis, about a third of my annual allowance for staff reverted to the treasury throughout my years in the Senate, and I know that such was the case, also, with senators from other of the small states.

Since my retirement I have noted that there has been another reclassification of the states, together with an increase of staff allowances all along the line—from the California senators, who apparently now receive $844,608 annually, to the smallest states, whose senators receive $413,082. (Senators have always been permitted to allocate their financial allowances as they saw fit, subject only to a ceiling placed on the salaries of the higher-paid staff members. They could have a large number of employees drawing modest compensation or concentrate much of their allowance on a small number of experienced, high-quality, higher-paid staffers.)

What are the duties that the modern, increased Senate staffs perform? The time of a considerable number of aides is used in handling work done for constituents or groups of constituents. I have already referred to this as "casework." As time goes on, different staffers become specialists in particular types of casework. Some master the laws pertaining to veterans, including disability allowances; others become especially familiar with visas and immigration problems; still others handle complaints from civil service employees. Thus, these staff aides develop expertise in given fields. They know exactly with whom to deal in the departments or agencies involved, and they are, indeed, typically far more knowledgeable than the senator himself about their special subject areas. If they run into difficulties on a case, they go to the senator, describe the situation to him, tell him what department official he should personally telephone—and, usually, exactly what he should say.

I think it important to describe this process, for there are many constituents who insist on talking directly with the senator in regard to their case or complaint, and who refuse to deal with his administrative assistant or any other subordinate. This is natural enough. The matter is important to them, and they do not feel they are getting proper attention unless they talk directly with their senator. It means, of course, that he has to take the time to respond personally—whether he is on the floor of the Senate or in committee or wherever he may be. But then, in fact, he turns the problem over, anyway, to that member of his staff who actually knows exactly how to pursue it.

I do not believe the Founding Fathers ever envisioned the cases and errands that would one day flood the offices of the federal government's legislative branch. In those times, they expected members would themselves study the issues and problems that come before the Congress; later, as staff personnel was added, it was provided on the basis of their handling the comparatively few complaints that were, in those days, received from individual constituents. Actually, however, the trend has been the other way around: the members themselves now spend a substantial part of their time on the telephone with constitutents, while staffers study the bills and amendments that are soon to be considered and on which they will ultimately brief the senators.

This situation is unfortunate. If constituents would be content, except in cases of emergency, to explain their problems to a staff member who knows exactly what information is needed in order to deal with the issues involved, they would get faster and better service, while the senator would have more time to study legislation personally. I can say this now that I am in retirement, but no senator or congressman would dare to make such a suggestion while in office, fearing his people might misunderstand, and feel that he did not want to bother with their troubles.

But the Senate personnel that has grown the most is not the personal staffs of senators (for these are at least subject to some restrictions as to size), but rather the committee staffs. There are no limits on these, except the amount of money that is appropriated for the use of the committee in its work—and, although there is frequently some grumbling from a few of the senior and conservative senators, "senatorial courtesy" (that phrase which covers a multitude of sins) results, by and large, in the Senate appropriating for each committee nearly all the money it requests. The growth of these staffs is most alarming because of the power and influence they exercise over legislation.

The ever-increasing stream of bills and resolutions now being introduced each session is, in a large measure, attributable to the similarly increasing army of committee staffers who unflaggingly devote their youthful energies to swelling the floodtide of proposed legislation, without the restraints that come from age and experience. Clearly, senators must have help in keeping pace with this proposed legislation, and that further augments both senatorial and committee staffs. Moreover, committee staffs have more and more arrogated to themselves the tasks of considering the merits of these bills, amending and redrafting many of them, and even attempting to dictate to the committees involved what action should be taken concerning them. Accordingly, not only have committee staffs been vastly enlarged, but so have their influence and power.

Each time the Senate has attempted a reorganization, to bring committee activities back under control of senators, the situation has been made worse. A few years ago an able, select committee was created for this purpose under the leadership of Senator Mike Monroney of Oklahoma and the late Senator Robert M. La Follette Jr. This committee worked long and hard to make it possible for senators to give more of their personal attention to their committee work. It was found that there were so many Senate committees that every senator was serving on five or six, or sometimes even seven or eight. Obviously, a senator could not possibly know what was going on in all the committees of which he was a member, much less participate in their deliberations.

The Monroney–La Follette committee recommended, and the Senate adopted, a complete reorganization. The number of committees was drastically reduced, from thirty-three to fifteen. Many minor committees were abolished and others were consolidated. The rule was adopted that no senator, regardless of his seniority, could serve on more than two major standing committees. But what happened? In cases in which the scattered jurisdiction of a lot of small committees had been brought under one major committee, that committee immediately split itself into subcommittees to deal with the various subjects that had been brought under the tent. This meant that each senator, instead of serving on seven or eight committees, found himself serving on seven or eight subcommittees. The main purpose of the reorganization was completely thwarted.

The mischief that was the unintended result of this reorganization went further. Practically every majority member of a standing committee became chairman of a subcommittee. As chairman of a subcommittee, he was not content to have one or two members of the regular staff of the full committee assigned to aid him, but insisted upon a separate staff of his own for the subcommittee—which in many cases grew until it had at least a half-dozen majority staffers and one minority staffer, plus stenographic assistance. In addition to all this, the chairmen of full committees, either of their own initiative or at the prompting of other majority members, would create special subcommittees to make studies of particular projects. These special committees, of course, all had to be staffed. In fact, the staffs did the work and came up with most of the ideas. In this way, the number of staffers mushroomed into proportions formerly undreamed of. One committee of which I was a member had a majority staff (counting personnel serving subcommittees, special committees, investigating committees, and "studies") of 109. In addition, the minority side of that committee was allowed eight staffers, plus three stenographers.

During the first year of my retirement, when I was considering the evils of an overstaffed Congress, I sought some estimates from Senate officials. They indicated to me that early budget requests in the Ninety-fourth Congress called for a total of committee staffs, in the Senate alone, of approximately 1,100. The overall total of senators' staffs varies from month to month, but it works out roughly to around 4,000, not counting staffs of offices of the Senate (such as those of the vice-president and the sergeant-at-arms), attachés, and staffs of the Senate as a whole, which would easily bring the total to 5,000. The total of staffs for both the Senate and the House has been estimated in the vicinity of 15,000.

Perhaps the most significant result of this staff population explosion is the torrent of legislative proposals that in recent years has practically overwhelmed the Senate. As I have mentioned, most of the work and most of the ideas come from the staffers. They are predominantly young men and women, fresh out of college and professional schools. They are ambitious, idealistic, and abounding with ideas.

Still further swelling this ever-increasing army is an additional force referred to on Capitol Hill as "interns." These are mostly undergraduates in our colleges who are brought to Washington for a number of months each year so that they may learn firsthand the workings of Congress. A portion of these students work in the offices of various senators and congressmen, but because in many instances their sponsors do not have space to accommodate them or time to supervise them, they are assigned to committees, which means an added influx of young eager beavers—to furnish ideas and inspiration for even more legislative proposals. Admittedly, there is much to be said for this internship scheme, but its existence does add to the horde of those dropping new ideas, new bills, new investigations, new studies into the laps of already overburdened members of the House and Senate. This has led, in the Senate at least, to a demand by senators for additional members of their own staff whom they could assign to attend committee hearings, conferences, and executive committee sessions, and who would then report back to them on what was taking place. Recently, the Senate has given each senator one additional staff member for every committee on which he serves. Thus, new staffers breed more new staffers—and the legislative process ever moves away from those elected by the people.

Let it be clearly understood that I do not wish to ridicule the work of earnest and sincere staffers. Many good and progressive ideas have and will come from these able people. But that Congress is greatly overstaffed and that overstaffing is detracting from its efficiency must, I believe, be the almost unanimous conclusion of observers who have had the opportunity to study the present situation firsthand. And it might be amazing if we knew how much legislation actually slides through committees, and reaches the floor for action, without previous consideration by those the people have chosen as their representatives—their senators and congressmen themselves.

Political portents point to a continued stepping up, rather than a toning down, of congressional staffs. Essentially, committee staffers are able, willing, and helpful. Also, they are not bashful. Quite often when an executive session of a committee is called to consider bills, it is found that the proposed bills have all been redrafted—and usually expanded—by the staff. Frequently, the staff has already released these bills in their new form to the press as "committee drafts," even though at this point no member of the committee has any knowledge of the redrafting. Naturally, senators on both sides are frequently incensed at this well-meant but high-handed procedure, and they object strenuously to some provisions that have been written into bills without their knowledge.

I recall one day sitting next to Senator Robert Griffin of Michigan in an executive session of a committee on which we both served, listening to a group of staff aides boldly disputing with members of the committee, including the chairman, and insisting their version of a bill was the result of careful study and should be accepted by the committee and reported to the Senate. Senator Griffin, grinning broadly, leaned over and whispered in my ear, "This committee spends most of its time arguing with its own staff." In that remark you have the whole story in a nutshell.

CHAPTER

VI

Of Lobbying and the Purity of Elections

Now and then an innocent man is sent to the legislature.
—*Kin Hubbard*

THE general term "lobbying" relates to the whole realm of outside influence exerted upon the Senate—its committees, individual senators, and staffs—by all kinds of pressure groups. If one were to carry this discussion to the ultimate, it would also involve campaign contributions, the various proposals for controlling them, and the whole history of Watergate, with its many revelations and ramifications. I shall not attempt this. Books could be written on the subject; in fact, have been written. I shall simply try to give some testimony on the overall subject, based on my own practical experience. Of necessity, it will be an oversimplification, but the whole problem is now so much in the public eye that it certainly requires comment.

One might think, in light of the present furor about corruption in the Congress and throughout the government, that questionable practices are a development that has come about only during the last few years. Actually, the problem, in some form, has been going on throughout most of the entire history of the Congress.

I recall vividly that during my first years as a member of the Senate, the Senate chamber had just been renovated and redecorated. It was decided that portraits of five senators famed in history should be placed in the Reception Room. A special committee was appointed to recommend the senators to be thus honored. After long deliberation, the committee recommended Webster, Clay, and Calhoun, the famous triumvirate in the period before the Civil War, and two of more recent date, namely, the elder La Follette and Robert A. Taft Sr.

When the committee recommendations reached the floor of the Senate, a heated debate, extending over several days, took place. The choice of Clay was attacked by several senators, who charged him with having accepted bribes from various sources. Clay was defended by both Kentucky senators, John Sherman Cooper and Thruston Morton. An even more vicious attack was made against Daniel Webster. Senator Paul Douglas of Illinois charged that Webster was venal, had accepted and even solicited gratuities, and while a senator had been an attorney for wealthy corporations and individuals in both Massachusetts and New York. He referred to letters in which Webster had urged his clients to hurry up with their retainers so that he could satisfy his many creditors. New Hampshire's senior senator, Styles Bridges, whose health was beginning to fail, was absent undergoing hospital treatment during this debate. So it fell to me to defend Webster, in a spirited exchange with Senator Douglas. I reminded the Senate that during the period of Webster's service, Senate sessions extended not more than three months out of a year; salaries were small, and practically all senators continued to engage in their usual vocations in their home states; that Webster, a practicing lawyer, was legitimately under retainer, not only by large and powerful clients, but by many others— including Dartmouth College, for which he fought one of the nation's most famous cases, still a landmark in legal history.

The point I want to emphasize here is that in the course of this extended debate it was revealed that throughout the years many senators had been accustomed to receiving substantial financial assistance from certain segments of society, particularly when they were running for reelection. (Several senators then present admitted frankly that they themselves were accustomed to receiving financial support from labor, farm organizations, or groups of individuals representing business interests. They insisted that there was nothing wrong in this practice.) Now, this debate occurred in the 1950s, and surprisingly, the news media gave so little attention to all these allegations that the whole episode passed unnoticed by the general public. It was only when the revelations and publicity following Watergate burst upon the country that probity became such a burning issue.

As a member of the Senate, I witnessed firsthand the unfolding of the entire Watergate scandal, even as I had seen somewhat similar episodes surface in preceding administrations. As I see it, there were three reasons for the tremendous impact of Watergate: first, the hostility of the news media toward a president they disliked; second, the scandal dramatically led, for the first time in our history, to the resignation of a president of the United States; and third, the public was shocked and amazed when it suddenly learned how many millions of dollars are spent to elect a president. It is noteworthy that every member of the special Senate committee that conducted the hearings and investigated the president, except its chairman, Senator Sam Ervin of North Carolina, had received and reported campaign contributions from one or more of the groups I have mentioned above. Indeed, practically every member of the whole Senate, including myself, had received and reported such contributions—although, of course, the amounts involved were "chicken feed" compared with the millions raised for a presidential campaign.

Throughout my earlier years in both the House and Senate, comparatively little attention was given by those bodies either to requiring the reporting of campaign receipts and expenditures or to placing limitations upon them. To be sure, there was a Committee on Elections, and candidates for the House and Senate were required to file a sketchy report on their campaign expenditures. "Sketchy" is an understatement. The required report was perfunctory, and the law was so full of holes that a moving van could pass through it. During those years, the only real check on campaign expenditures was by the states. Be it said to the credit of New Hampshire that more than twenty years ago its legislature passed a strict election law, and in it our legislature made an earnest attempt to plug all loopholes. It required the filing of reports by candidates both before and after primary and general elections, enumerating all contributions and their sources, as well as all expenditures and to whom paid. It placed a limitation on the amount that could be spent by candidates for various offices, including governor, U.S. senator, congressman, and others. It limited the amount that any individual could contribute to a candidate and made it unlawful for corporations and organized labor to make political contributions.

This last-cited New Hampshire provision appears in subsequent federal enactments, as well as in those of other states, but labor has been successful in circumventing this law by forming COPE (Committee on Political Education), which backs prolabor candidates with both financial and organizational support. This is a clever and practical device, which the courts have found to be perfectly legitimate, because the contributions are supposedly voluntary and not collected from union dues. In contrast to labor, business and management have, on the whole, shown themselves to be inept in similarly protecting their interests. Organizations such as the National Association of Manufacturers and the National Chamber of Commerce have complacently listened to endless hours of oratory about the free-enterprise system and the role of business, big and small, in providing jobs and maintaining a strong America. However, their meetings are attended by their own membership, so they are virtually talking to themselves. Business executives have done little to select and encourage congressional candidates who would give fair consideration to the problems of the business segment. To be sure, big business, through its officers and stockholders, has made contributions—mostly in the form of purchasing blocks of seats at $100-a-plate fund-raising dinners—but the fly in that ointment is the fact that in many if not most cases, they purchase an equal number of seats from both political parties, apparently having the naive notion that, with a foot in each camp, they will get a fair break from the Congress, regardless of which political party dominates it. Really, it was only with the revelations made by Maurice Stans and others of the huge sums of money raised and spent in the reelection of Richard Nixon that an aroused public forced a frightened Congress to undertake election reform.

In my opinion, the "reform" measures adopted by the Ninety-third Congress were so impractical, ineffective, and deceptive as to border on the ridiculous. I voted against every one of them, and I make no apology whatever for those votes. The experience of my own four campaigns for the House and four campaigns for the Senate, as well as my observation of the campaigns of others, including those of presidential candidates, has convinced me that no limitation by law on how much a candidate may spend will ever hold water. Such limitations only serve to drive political expenditures underground. Worse yet, the idea that we can purify politics by taking many millions of dollars, as we did in 1976, from the taxpayers' pockets to help finance political candidates is not only absurd, but a shocking misuse of public money. If a rich man or one with rich friends is running against a poor man with limited financial support, the great Solon himself could not devise a law that would equalize their chances. That is why I consider it useless to put a limit on what a candidate can spend. A way can always be found to circumvent a fixed limitation.

To me, the solution is as simple as it is direct: provide that every candidate for major office should account publicly and file with the Congress—or, in the case of state office, with the secretary of state—at the end of each month of his candidacy, an indication of how much he has spent or how much has been spent in his behalf and the amount of future expenditures for which he has obligated himself. Punishment should be provided for failure to file or for falsifying these reports—punishment so drastic as to put the fear of God into every political candidate. The punishment might well be the removal of the violator's name from the ballot and that, moreover, he be declared ineligible for public office for a period of years, if the slightest misstatement or illegality is found. Few candidates would dare to take a chance in the face of such a penalty, particularly in view of the fact that they could legally spend *any* amount, as long as they were willing for the people to know precisely what was being spent. It is my belief that if the public is fully informed throughout the progress of a campaign (not after it is over) as to the sums being expended by each candidate, the people can be trusted to see to it that public office is not put on the auction block and sold to the highest bidder. And the adoption of such a formula would prevent all this silly tommyrot about purifying elections by financing them out of the public treasury.

Actually, as far as Congress is concerned, this whole problem could probably have been avoided if each member had followed one simple code of ethics and if that code had been reinforced by the rules of both houses and written, when necessary, into the statutes. Any member of Congress, or any candidate or prospective candidate for membership, should have at all times a campaign treasurer or, adopting the New Hampshire designation, a fiscal agent. Any contribution received at any time, whether in campaigns or between elections, should immediately be submitted to him and duly reported jointly by him and the candidate when the candidacy for election or reelection becomes official. If the member decides not to seek reelection or the prospective candidate concludes not to file, the money should be returned to the donors, except perhaps for a prorated amount of what may have been used for polls or other expenses in making a determination on whether to become a candidate. This course I have followed consistently, immediately transferring all contributions to the campaign treasurer and having him acknowledge them by letter to the donors. If anyone wants to contribute secretly, it should not be accepted. This procedure affords practically airtight protection against any charge of misconduct. Had it been generally practiced, the people's image of their Congress would today be far different than it is.

Of course, there is one other vexing question, and that is gifts other than money. This becomes a question of the value of the item which has been given. I remember a White House luncheon when someone asked Dwight Eisenhower what rule he followed with regard to the many presents showered upon him as president. He replied that he made it a general practice not to accept anything that could not be eaten or drunk within forty-eight hours. At that time he was stocking his Gettysburg farm, to which he was planning to retire, and I was amused a few weeks later to read that a farmers' organization had presented him with two thoroughbred cows. I tried to imagine how even a president could consume two cows in forty-eight hours—unless he called in the whole Congress and had a barbecue.

Turning to the pressures on Congress that come under the general head of "lobbying," I find considerable interest in this subject on the part of many people. There seems to be a strong impression that Congress has many masters, when it should have only one—the constituents back home. This is another conception that has helped build up the widespread distrust our people have for their elected representatives. There seems to be a notion that one part of the Congress is financed and owned by organized labor and the other part by big business. In the main, this is fallacious, but it must be admitted that there is some foundation for it. Labor and business are, however, by no means the only groups that are constantly seeking to bring pressure upon senators and congressmen. It would be impossible to enumerate the organizations that are constantly engaged in trying to dominate the Congress. Many of these organizations have no personal or financial axes to grind, but only a sincere (and sometimes almost fanatical) belief regarding the direction the nation should take or what elements of society should prevail.

Some of these groups are liberal, such as Common Cause, the Committee for a Better Congress, the American Civil Liberties Union, the League of Women Voters, and all the so-called "consumer organizations" headed by their patron saint, Mr. Nader. Others are conservative, like the Americans for Constitutional Action, the National Association of Manufacturers, the General Contractors of America, and various tax organizations. You can add to the foregoing: service organizations dedicated to the welfare of veterans; the Farm Bureau, the Grange, and the Farmers' Union, pressing their various views on agriculture and the food problem; the proabortionists and the antiabortionists; and those who long for prayer in the schools, as well as those who abhor it. These and many other groups are ever hammering at the doors of Congress.

It could be noted in passing how pressures on Congress have increased over the years and how the methods of approaching our lawmakers have been refined and perfected. I have already emphasized that the whole Washington scene, including Capitol Hill, has changed enormously since I worked there as a staffer over half a century ago. Then, those whose private interests or convictions were being affected by legislation were not located within the capital city itself. They had to make their approaches by mail or, if the matter were of enough importance, by sending a representative to Washington to present their views to committees and individual members. That situation has utterly changed. Business, labor, the farmers, the veterans, and literally scores of national lobbies maintain permanent headquarters in Washington, with substantial staffs and skilled lawyers or other representatives, in easy reach of Capitol Hill.

For instance, if one wants to realize how potent the influence of labor has become, one has only to take a look around Washington. Facing the Capitol and the Senate office buildings is the five-million-dollar, ultramodern, marble-faced Teamsters Union Building. (Dave Beck said he put it there because "Congress would bear watching.") From his penthouse on top of a four-million-dollar headquarters, the president of AFL-CIO looks down on the White House. Opposite the Hotel Statler is the Bakery Workers' six-million-dollar building. Opposite the Mayflower Hotel are the Operating Engineers—in a two-million-dollar edifice. The Machinists (a two-and-a-half-million-dollar structure) are near Dupont Circle, and the Electrical Workers occupy a mere $750,000 shack on 15th Street. It is no crime to be big, but power requires watching and regulation—whether it be big government, big business, or big labor.

Although instances of corruption of labor leaders or of Communist domination of unions have been few, all union members are entitled to have their rights safeguarded. It was their dues that provided the palatial mansions and swimming pools for Beck and Jimmy Hoffa, swank air-conditioned homes for other presidents, and Cadillacs for many union officials. "History," said Voltaire, "is only the patter of silken slippers descending the stairs to the thunder of hobnail boots climbing up from below." The hobnail boots of labor are sound and strong, but some of the leaders have reached the "silken slipper" stage.

I have said that methods of approach to influencing legislation have in recent years been refined and perfected. Skillful, modern lobbyists no longer haunt the offices of members or buttonhole them in corridors. They know very well that this approach is an annoyance, and hence counterproductive. This is particularly true with senators who represent large constituencies, serve on many committees, and are always pressed for time. Nowadays, most lobbyists appear in the public hearings held by committees on the subject in which they are interested, and then, instead of trying personally to reach individual senators, they send the word back home to all their members in the states and arrange to deluge senatorial offices with letters from constituents. However, even this practice is fast losing its effectiveness. When three or four hundred letters are received the same day, all of them almost identically worded and all of them referring to a bill by its number, senators and their staffs recognize instantly, of course, that this rash of letters is not spontaneous on the part of the writers, but has been stimulated by some organization. In many cases these are clearly mere form letters, prepared, typed, and requiring only the signature of the sender. Naturally, this sort of communication does not impress a veteran senator. He dictates a form answer to what is obviously a form appeal or protest, and turns it over to his staff. One independent letter, written by the sender and representing his own convictions, is likely to receive more attention than a whole mailbag full of the other type.

It is really unfortunate and somewhat unjust that the term "lobbyist" has acquired such a sinister connotation. In the main, those who represent various interests, as well as those who are presenting diverse social and economic viewpoints to the Congress, are performing a legitimate and necessary function. Indeed, lobbyists' legal knowledge and technical skills are frequently helpful to committees in framing legislation. I recall that during my service on the Senate Commerce Committee, which has jurisdiction over all forms of transportation and communication, there were many instances when the representatives of airlines, railroads, and truckers were of practical aid in helping to draft bills and amendments. Although they openly and frankly represented the interests of their clients, these lobbyists were always ready to be of assistance in a disinterested manner. I remember particularly how cooperative the representatives of the three major radio and television networks were in helping us lay the foundations for our Public

Broadcasting System which, to a certain extent, was predictably going to compete with the commercial networks for audiences. To an even greater degree, those who represent social, political, and religious organizations are useful in filling a need for presenting the special viewpoints of their members to the Congress.

The ever-shortening time that members of Congress, particularly senators, can spend in their home states among their constitutents is an unfortunate development. In my earlier years in the Senate, we averaged about eight months in Washington and four months at home each year. Now, recesses rarely total more than a month and a half annually. It is important to realize that, contrary to popular conception, Congress functions just as much in recess as during its sessions. There is good reason for this. Congress is the bridge between Main Street and Washington. One of the prime duties of its members is to bring the views of folks at home to the career workers—the professionals of government—who spend their years in the towering buildings on the Potomac and rarely, if ever, rub elbows with the people. Furthermore, Congress is a barometer to gauge and analyze the opinions of the people and—more important—always to be aware of their needs. It is just as desirable for a senator to be home four months of the year as it is for him to be in the Senate the other eight.

I think wistfully of my first years in the Senate, when there was more opportunity for time at home. I used to advertise and hold regular "office hours" throughout New Hampshire in nonelection years. During one recess, my staff and I held sessions in 25 cities and towns, traveled 2,300 miles (the distance from Manchester, New Hampshire to Salt Lake City, Utah), held 701 personal interviews, and in addition were visited by 296 young people from our schools. And, of course, it was impossible to count or include the men and women who talked with me informally on the streets and in restaurants during that interval.

Although our people are sometimes prone to be discouraged and disheartened by the human weaknesses and shortcomings of some of their chosen representatives in Washington, upon whom they depend to set an example of integrity and morality, let me mention a bit of philosophy that has reassured me through the many years during which I have watched, from a close vantage point, that which is bad and that which is good in the halls of Congress. It is amazing that throughout history, the greatest achievements for liberty and human rights have ultimately emerged from the clash and conflicts within assemblies of very human and, many times, very selfish men. I think, for example, of the men who comprised the convention that finally succeeded in writing the Constitution of the United States. That convention was made up of rich, landowning, slaveholding southern planters and of affluent shipbuilders and traders of the North. Not one common worker or artisan was a member of that convention, and yet, they finally wrote a Constitution and a Bill of Rights which, with the sole exception of their failure to deal with Negro slavery, have been for two centuries the bulwark of human liberty and equal justice under the law. I think also of the barons who gathered on the plains of Runnymede, every one of them feudal lords, deriving their power and riches from the serfs whom they trampled beneath their feet in their various domains. Yet, they were fearful of the tyranny of a king, and selfish and self-serving as they were, they produced the Magna Carta, which eventually destroyed their own dominance and made men free throughout the English-speaking world.

Sometimes in the solemnity of a funeral service, when I hear intoned those ancient words from First Corinthians:

> It is sown in corruption; it is raised in incorruption:
> It is sown in dishonor; it is raised in glory:
> It is sown in weakness; it is raised in power

I think of the town meetings I have attended, of the city councils I have seen, of the legislatures in which I have served, and of all my years amidst the conflict and the turmoil of the House and Senate of the United States. There could be no such thing as government "of the people, by the people, for the people" if it were not for the comforting fact that whatever selfish motives, prejudice, and passion may characterize individuals, when they meet in bodies to enact laws and rules their ultimate collective judgment moves toward what is just and right. Thus has progress been made through the years and over the centuries. As Christopher Morley well said, "There is no squabbling so violent as that between people who accepted an idea yesterday and those who will accept the same idea tomorrow."

CHAPTER

VII

Where the Spotlight Falls

We live under a government of men and morning newspapers.
—*Wendell Phillips*

THE second half of the twentieth century has witnessed the creation of a "royal family" in the American democracy. By royal family, I do not mean any particular family—not the Kennedys, not the Roosevelts, not the Rockefellers. I am referring, rather, to whoever may be the tenants of the White House at any given time. They include the president, his wife, his children, his collateral relatives, his ox, his ass —and even his dog. (Remember the famous Fala of Roosevelt's day, transported halfway around the world by a destroyer; Johnson, accused of brutality for lifting his pet beagles by the ears; and Nixon's Checkers, a subject of one of history's corniest speeches?)

The fact that in recent years the attention of the public and the news media has become riveted upon the White House is not really a subject for jest or irony, because it has seriously impaired—indeed almost destroyed—the capacity and effectiveness of that all-important branch of our republic—the Congress. In the Congress reposes the people's government: senators elected by the people in every one of fifty states; representatives elected by the people in 435 districts throughout the land. If the Congress is allowed to become weak, ineffective, or corrupt, then the people's government fails. This fundamental precept was laid down in no uncertain terms by Thomas Jefferson when he said:

I know no safe depository of the ultimate powers of the society but the people themselves; and if we think them not enlightened enough to exercise their control with a wholesome discretion, the remedy is not to take it from them, but to inform their discretion by education.

Yet today, two centuries after Mr. Jefferson, Congress, the elected representative branch of government, has reached its low ebb in effectiveness, devotion to duty, and (in many cases) integrity. It has also reached a low point in public esteem. Obviously, Congress is now "no safe depository of the ultimate powers of society." And just as clearly, the reason lies, still in the words of Jefferson, in the fact that "the people themselves" are, for the present at least, "not enlightened enough to exercise their control with a wholesome discretion." The same authority makes the remedy equally clear: "to inform their discretion by education."

Absorbed in the glory and the glamor of the presidency, too many of our people have become indifferent as to who represents them in the Congress and at the state and local levels. Gone are the days when people turned out in substantial numbers to see and listen to candidates for governor, for senator, for congressman, and for state and local offices. Life was quite different then (days not so far removed but that many of us senior citizens recall them vividly). Automobiles were few in number and not too dependable for prolonged journeys. Air travel was in its infancy. Broad throughways had not supplanted railroads. Only the wealthy and the leisurely traveled extensively. Mobile homes and campers had not yet made nomads of the American people. The vast majority traveled only on rare occasions, and depended upon the resources of their own community for enlightenment, entertainment, and amusement. There were no television screens, and people actually read books. The coffee break had not become an institution, and people at work welcomed the brief diversion of meeting, greeting, and sizing up candidates; and in the evening they turned out for the old-fashioned political rallies.

Radio and television have changed all this. Today the focus of public attention is overwhelmingly on the White House. Newscasters and commentators need not, however, assume the entire responsibility for this. Naturally they give the people what interests them. And what does interest the people? They want to look into the Oval Office, or perhaps the Rose Garden, to see and hear the president greeting foreign dignitaries. They want to view the president addressing the Congress. They want to watch the First Lady—observe her clothes and her hairdo and listen to her opinions on such subjects as whether she approves of abortion or is intolerant of young people using "pot." They are particularly interested in the president's children and how they behave. Occasionally, they may tune in on a panel discussion by governors, senators, and congressmen—unless there happens to be a football game or a golf match going on at the same time. But only the president can command prime time on all channels.

The inevitable result of all this is that large numbers have become indifferent regarding who represents them in the Congress, and they are uninformed about those who seek to represent them. If proof is needed of this, one has only to talk with political workers whose task it is to try to "get out the vote." They will testify that it is comparatively easy to induce voters to go to the polls every four years in presidential elections (indeed, many flock there of their own volition), but in "off-year," nonpresidential elections, when only senators, congressmen, and state and local officials are being chosen, it is like pulling teeth trying to drag people to the polls. Thus, it may reasonably be contended that the American electorate must bear a heavy portion of the blame for the inadequacies and weaknesses of their Congress.

On the other hand, the constant deterioration of the Congress, which has been taking place for a long time but has not been fully realized until recent times, cannot be laid wholly at the door of the news media, the public, or anyone other than the members of that body itself. The men and women who comprise the Senate and House of Representatives are the masters of their own fates. For the most part they are persons of higher than average intelligence, and most of them have spent years on Capitol Hill. Surely they are, or should be, fully aware of the pitfalls that lie in the path of every national legislator. They need no code of ethics hanging on their office walls to tell them what is just and fair, what is honorable or dishonorable. This is true not only in the conduct of the nation's business, but also with respect to their own compensation, patronage, allowances, and perquisites. Moreover, the members of both bodies always know full well what schemes are going on and what their leadership and the chairmen of major committees are up to. If by their silence they acquiesce in improper practices that have been taking place, they cannot evade their share of accountability.

Of course the fact is that "when the cat's away, the mice will play." For a period of years now, the attention of the country, the glare of publicity, the credit for achievements, and the blame for misfortune and misconduct have focused on the nation's chief executive. We have seen one president forced to relinquish all hope for reelection because of the disastrous and unpopular war in Vietnam, another driven from office in disgrace, cabinet officers prosecuted, and important officers in the executive branch imprisoned. During all this time, the Congress has enjoyed a happy anonymity, procrastinating and stalling, pushing vital decisions onto the back burner, taking so-called "inspection trips" to all parts of the world at the public's expense, and constantly increasing staffs, allowances, and their own direct and indirect compensation—all this almost unnoticed by either the people or the press—until some relatively recent revelations. In justice, it should emphatically be said that a large number in both houses of Congress have, indeed, vigorously protested wrongdoing and improprieties, and have tried to maintain personal standards that would entitle our national legislative bodies to the respect of the citizenry. However, these individuals have failed to muster even sufficient support to command attention, to say nothing of achieving reforms.

It is difficult to acquire even a bird's-eye view of "what makes Congress tick" unless one is given a general understanding of some of the problems that face a member of either house from the first week after he is sworn in—and many of which, in some form, remain with him throughout all his years as a congressman or a senator, until he goes to his final reward or until he fastens his briefcase for the last time and leaves Capitol Hill forever.

Thirty years ago, when I came to Washington as a fledgling congressman, I expected to face difficult decisions. I assumed, however, that all one had to do was study the questions thoroughly and vote one's convictions fearlessly. But it is not that simple. We seldom, in fact, get a chance to "vote our convictions." When the time comes to vote yea or nay on a piece of legislation, it is almost never all black or all white. Usually it is a mottled gray. We vote for a bill because we decide it has more good in it than bad, or against it because we decide it has more bad than good. Often we are in a quandary before we determine our vote and then, afterward, have our doubts and qualms about it.

It is thrilling to read or listen to the defiant utterances of statesmen proclaiming rigid adherence to their convictions. They seem stern and unbending, declaring that they will never yield so much as a millimeter. I have been reading some of these pronouncements since I left the Senate—usually by senators fairly new to the scene. Yet, they must learn, as we all did, that in the last analysis, life (in or out of the Senate) is a series of compromises.

You do not abandon your goals or cease striving for them, but you learn to take what you can get, and come back for more the next Congress. You must make compromises in your committees, compromises on the floor of the Senate, compromises in conference with the House—and sometimes compromises with the president, in order to give him a bill that he will sign. By the same token, if you consider a measure too costly or dangerous or ineffective, you beat it if you can—and maim it if you can't. Above all, you learn to roll with the punches and accept setbacks and disappointments with neither bitterness nor despondency. If your political party is constantly in the minority (as mine has been throughout my years in the Senate), so that you are always outnumbered, can never be chairman of a committee or subcommittee, can never select what measures shall be heard or even set a time for their hearing, you learn to live with that, too. And, gradually, you learn what should be the role of the minority: not to oppose blindly every program presented, not to sit in sullen apathy while the juggernaut rolls over you—but, rather, to meet each issue strictly on its merits and strive to set an example of constructive statesmanship.

If one were to attempt an essay on "The Making of a Senator," it could have one dominant theme and only one—that which I have just mentioned: to learn to accept defeats without rancor and victories without exaltation, and never to give up. Many a new member comes to the Senate with a chip on his shoulder, convinced that his way is the only right way and that anyone who disagrees must be a public enemy. That is the first belief that he must unlearn, for the Senate would soon cease to be a deliberative body if it contained too many members with that attitude. So the longer one serves in the Senate, the more tolerant one becomes of the opinions of others. The Senate still remembers the prayer of its late, beloved chaplain, Peter Marshall: "Lord, when we are wrong, make us willing to change. And when we are right, make us easy to live with."

To illustrate the occasional necessity to compromise, may I be permitted to draw from personal experience. During my earlier years in the Senate, we were continuously battling over federal aid to education. I was one of those who long wanted a chance to vote for a bill that would put federal aid straight into the school districts, under a simple formula providing no federal control or creating no federal agency to eat up part of the funds, and leaving each district free to use the money for its own particular needs—teachers' salaries, construction, or whatever. For three Congresses, I offered my own plan in the form of an amendment to the bill establishing federal aid to education. My amendment provided that a small percentage (2 percent at the start) of the personal federal income taxes collected from each state be returned to that state, earmarked for education. My approach, I contended, involved plain common sense and stark simplicity. No complicated formula for distribution would be necessary. Hardly an additional government clerk would be needed to compute the share of each state; it would give rise to no huge department of planners in Washington and no army of inspectors and enforcers to travel through the states. But bureaucracy does not work that way and, at least in recent years, neither does the Senate. During the last decade, it has seemed to me that every two years has added to the number of stargazing visionaries in that body. They scoff at any of us who are so benighted as to believe those people who have the interests of our school children most at heart are their fathers and mothers or that these same fathers and mothers, plus teachers, local school authorities, and parent-teacher associations, have sufficient intelligence to expend their own tax dollars wisely.

In 1965, for the third time in six years, my amendment went down to defeat, and even though Senator Case of South Dakota and others had joined as cosponsors, we mustered only thirty-three votes. Then, what was I to do? Heaven knows, I hated to vote for the overall bill. Its cost was two-and-a-half billion dollars a year at the start, and much of this amount went for the frills and furbelows rather than the essentials of education. It included supplementary education centers, libraries, research, added personnel for state boards of education, teacher-training courses, college-dormitory loans, and so on. The formula for distributing the money among the states was not only complicated but, in my opinion, unfair. It involved multiplying the low-income families by the average state expenditure per pupil. Thus, states and districts benefited without regard for their own resources—some of the richest receiving more than some of the poorest.

Nevertheless, there were impelling reasons for not voting against the bill. Although laden with federal expense, it was not so completely shackled by federal control as some of its predecessors. Under it, at least 94 percent of the school districts in the United States would receive some direct aid, mostly in the form of impacted area funds. To be sure, the people of New Hampshire, under this bill, would pay four-and-a-half million dollars and get back only two-and-a-half million—but New Hampshire was at that time paying its share of a billion dollars for Appalachia and getting nothing; it was paying its part for mass transit in the big cities of America and getting nothing; it was obligated to pay toward nearly half a billion dollars for a Washington subway system and millions more to beautify the Potomac, and getting nothing. The inescapable fact was that I had fought six years for the kind of federal aid I could support with a clear conscience and failed, and clearly this bill was the best which one could hope to get. The education of our youth was, I felt, the most vital need of our generation—far more important than the billions we were wasting on many other programs—and I just could not stand by and see federal aid to education, again, go down the drain. So, despite all its imperfections, I held my nose and voted for it.

This is an example of the dilemma that frequently confronts your senators, forcing them to bite the bullet and, reluctantly, support a measure because it is that or nothing. What makes this the most striking example is that in this fast-moving Space Age, Congress had for years been killing time on educating our youth, and as Thoreau so well put it, "As if you could kill time without injuring eternity."

But let me return, briefly, to the matter of public assessment of the Congress. It should be borne in mind that, usually, the higher the office, the more quickly any misconduct or improprieties are detected and become general knowledge. Presidents, cabinet members, and even senators operate in the public eye, and although some of them, who have the advantage of a friendly press and the support of a majority of the Congress, may be accorded a measure of temporary immunity, at least during their terms of office, they are bound, sooner or later (and usually sooner), to become the victims of their misdeeds or transgressions. A considerable portion of public officialdom, on the other hand, enjoys a certain anonymity, where the exposure of human frailties and shortcomings is long delayed. For instance, it takes many years for a member of the House of Representatives to obtain enough seniority to become a powerful committee chairman. The comparative obscurity of those years remains with a congressman when he has reached the top, and the attention of the public is rarely drawn to how he uses his power once he has attained it. As a member of the House, I often marveled at the bold and arbitrary manner in which committee chairmen exercised their authority and attained their ends. Let me cite three examples, just in passing.

The first is an incident that directly involved me—and over which I still find myself chuckling. Senator Bridges was striving to secure the Pease Air Force Base for New Hampshire. He was opposed by his colleague Senator Tobey and by the congressman from New Hampshire's First District. However, I as congressman from the Second District was in favor of Bridges's efforts, and one morning he called me and asked that I appear before the House Armed Services Committee and offer testimony in favor of the base's establishment. Bridges, because of his long service and influence, had the support of Carl Vinson, the powerful chairman of that committee. When I appeared in the anteroom of the committee, I was abruptly informed by a staff member that I could not enter, because the committee was in executive session. At that point, Chairman Vinson and Senator Bridges came through the room to enter the committee. The staff member informed Vinson that I was a congressman from New Hampshire and wanted to testify. Vinson turned to me and sternly reiterated that it was an executive session and I could not come in. At this point, Bridges whispered in his ear, whereupon Vinson said, "Wait a minute, are you testifying *for* the air force base?" I said, "Yes, Mr. Chairman." He beamed and replied, "In that case, come in, come in." He welcomed me and introduced me as the initial witness.

The second case in point relates to the period of my membership on the House Appropriations Committee. The chairman, although a fairly elderly man, had been a boxer in his youth and always kept himself in good physical condition. I was present one day when a junior member of the committee angered him by the manner and persistence of his opposition. The chairman promptly knocked him down and blackened both his eyes; the members of the committee had to separate them. The incident, however, never got into print.

And thirdly, when Carl Vinson retired, he was succeeded as chairman of the Armed Services Committee by my good friend Mendel Rivers of South Carolina. Although Rivers may have dealt more smoothly with his committee associates, he unabashedly made use of his power to pack South Carolina, and particularly his own congressional district, so full of military installations that it was a wonder to me they did not have to tear down a few schools and churches to make room for them.

These examples will show how ruthlessly veteran House chairmen could, through the years, use their power and get away with it, provided they kept their own membership reasonably happy by doling out a few favors to them.

For many years Wilbur Mills, chairman of the Committee on Ways and Means, and Wayne Hays, chairman of House Administration, ruled their respective domains with iron hands, untroubled by either the press or the public, until they got themselves scandalously involved with the fairer sex, which tore the cover off the whole show.

The Senate, probably because it has always been more under the public's scrutiny, has never been so bold and high-handed in its procedures. No Senate chairman, with his committee constantly covered by the press, would ever be so openly arbitrary, nor would senatorial courtesy permit it. Furthermore, the public censure of Joseph McCarthy in the 1950s for violating Senate rules in his conduct toward other senators and the public, as well as the censure of Thomas Dodd in the 1960s for misuse of campaign funds, have left their mark upon the Senate and served as a warning to members of that body that they must keep their houses in order.

One factor that has contributed in no small measure to the loss of congressional prestige has been the tendency of candidates seeking election or reelection to be so unrestrained in their promises of federal benefits to various segments of our population that when the time comes to make good, they must either fail to keep the promises or be so prodigal and lavish in their use of public monies and public credit as to heat up inflation, destroy private employment, and worsen the lot of the unfortunates they are pretending to help. But this is a point I shall reserve for development in a later chapter.

Those who are inclined to rest their hopes on the panaceas of politicians could profit from this thank-you letter for a package sent to a European family:

> Please send more of those pills. We didn't know what they were until Cousin Lempi, who studied English, read the name for us. Then we gave them all to Uncle Paul, who suffers from rheumatism. He feels better now, and says it's the best medicine he ever took. If you don't remember the name of the pills, they're called Life Savers.

CHAPTER

VIII

Nationally Known Senators — and Others

I would rather have men ask, after I am dead, why I
have no monument than why I have one.

—Cato the Elder

HAVING touched, in the foregoing chapter, upon certain of the problems
with which every senator and congressman is faced and which serve
to complicate his life, it would seem appropriate perhaps, before leaving the subject, to identify some others that are not ordinarily visible
to the outside observer. Those I shall mention here will particularly
concern the Senate, where I spent the bulk of my years.

In the first place, a lawmaker must always play a dual role. He is
a representative of his constituents, but he is also a politician, and he
must strive to maintain a proper balance between the two functions
involved. If he neglects to stay close to his own people or to keep his
lines of communication open to them at all times; if, instead, he is forever seeking publicity nationally, making speeches in various parts of
the country, and traveling constantly from one end of the land to the
other, his career may be short and sweet. He may make a noise in the
Senate and get attention from the press, but his people back home
want first claim on their senator. It is quite possible, on the other hand,
for a member to devote so much of his time and energy to "mending
his political fences" with the electorate that he fails to be active and
vocal enough in the deliberations of the Senate. In such cases the press
gallery is prone to write him off early in his service, and he may find
that regardless of how great his seniority and influence may grow, he

gets little attention from the newsmen and is unlikely to be invited to participate in "Meet the Press" or other nationally televised discussions. How, then, can a senator perform outstandingly in this dual capacity—walking the tightrope between the requirements of his constituency and the general duties of his office?

Ever since parliaments and legislative bodies have existed, it has been a moot question as to whether a representative, in casting his vote, should follow the wishes of his constituents or his own personal convictions. There is a classic discussion of this question that has been repeated, quoted, and often criticized down through the years. In 1774, upon being elected from Bristol to the British Parliament, Edmund Burke declared himself on this point to the electors who had chosen him:

> Certainly, gentlemen, it ought to be the happiness . . . of a representative, to live in the strictest union, the closest correspondence . . . with his constituents. Their wishes ought to have great weight with him; their opinions high respect; their business unremitted attention. . . . But, his unbiased opinion, his mature judgment, his enlightened conscience, he ought not to sacrifice to [them]. . . . Your representative owes you, not his industry only, but his judgment; and he betrays, instead of serving you if he sacrifices it to your opinions.

(It is noteworthy that perhaps Mr. Burke's declaration of principle did not set too well upon the people of Bristol. At any rate, he was not their choice in the next election, although he soon thereafter returned to Parliament—from another constituency—and he had, of course, a long and distinguished career in the House of Commons. And here, to use a trite and worn-out expression that appears so often in party platforms, I must "point with pride" to the fact that the people of New Hampshire have had, in my case, more understanding than did the electors of Bristol, in Burke's. On occasions after I voted on highly controversial matters upon which my letters from home had been overwhelmingly the other way, I gave the reasons for my votes in my regular "Reports," reviewing the evidence that had been presented and explaining the details of the bill—and in one of these newspaper "Reports," indeed, I actually quoted the words of Edmund Burke. Admittedly, I received a few critical letters in response, but to my pleasant surprise, I received more in which the writers indicated that while some of them still disagreed with me, they understood my reasoning and felt I had done my duty as I saw it, which was all that they expected. This happened, I am happy to say, many times during my service—and it shows the kind of people we have in New Hampshire.)

It is true that your senators, having available firsthand expert evidence on many issues, may at times be better equipped to form a judgment than are those who are remote from the scene. This certainly does not mean, however, that all the wisdom in this country originates on the banks of the Potomac. To the contrary, I have found many times more real, down-to-earth common sense in thoughtful people back home than I have heard within the halls of Congress. Let me give you just one simple example. In the summer of 1967, I received a letter from a housewife whose husband was making a very moderate salary, whose taxes and costs of living were jumping, and whose children were reaching college age. Her closing words, straight from the heart, were more eloquent and meaningful than those of any speech I ever heard in the Senate:

> Where does the government get its money? From the vacations we
> could never take, the movies we never saw, the restaurant dinners
> we never ate, the clothes we never bought, and the savings we
> haven't got.

What a scorching indictment of uncontrolled government, of a runaway economy, and of an unfair tax system that caters to the very rich, coddles the very poor, and is slowly but surely crushing "middle America." Because her husband's modest salary was undoubtedly above the designated "poverty level," food stamps were not for her, government scholarships were not for her children; and probably not being one of a "minority group," a score of glittering federal programs were not available to her. Instead she and her husband had to scrimp and save, and pay the freight—city, state, and federal taxes—and the inflated prices of the family food at the supermarket.

I repeated the splendid, ringing words of this constituent on the floor of the U.S. Senate not once, but several times. I was wasting my breath. The vast majority of the present-day Senate, devotees of the "Great Society," are interested, I am afraid, only in giving out goodies. They seem utterly indifferent to the middle class, who are struggling desperately to support their families and, at the same time, to carry the tax burden that a heedless government keeps heaping upon them. That is one of the many reasons I came home from the Senate with a heavy heart.

The above incident emphasizes the need of a senator to keep open his lines of communication with those he represents. This is infinitely more important than having a press secretary release announcements to home newspapers about federal grants the senator has helped to obtain, bills he has introduced, and speeches he has made. In earlier days, when the country was more agricultural and less industrial, and much more sparsely populated, your representatives in Washington had much more direct contact with their constituents.

I have vivid recollections of how, seventy years ago, when I was a lad on a farm, our congressman used to come periodically to visit the farmers. He was quite a character! He himself owned a farm, with a few head of dairy cattle and, more important, several well-bred horses that he raced at the fairs. I remember especially his calling on my father, going through the barn, feeling of the cows and commenting on them. On these occasions, he affected carelessness of dress, wearing high leather boots, usually with one pant leg tucked in and the other hanging loose. People were somewhat less sophisticated in those days, but they were intelligent and shrewd, and I doubt if they were greatly fooled by the congressman's posture. Nevertheless, they were glad to see him, and we youngsters were as thrilled as if the president had called on us.

I was particularly impressed by the other congressman from New Hampshire in those bygone days: a legendary figure, the famous "Tall Pine of the Merrimack," Cyrus Sulloway, whose life-size portrait still adorns the capitol at Concord—nearly seven feet tall! Senator Moses used to tell me how Cy Sulloway would stand in front of the Eagle

Hotel in Concord on convention days, reaching his long arm over the heads of the people about him, clasping the hands of his constituents. One of them, Moses recalled, told Sulloway his name. "Why of course I remember you, Mr. Pike," he responded. "Are you still driving that white horse of yours?" "Oh yes, congressman," said the man, flattered and pleased. Moses, then a young reporter, was much impressed and asked the congressman, "How did you know he drove a white horse?" Sulloway chuckled and said, "He had white hairs all over his coat."

Nowadays, with the ever-increasing density of population and with Congress almost continuously in session, members must find other and less direct means of reaching their constituents. At the beginning of my second two-year term in the House, I started writing regular weekly "Reports," sending them not only to the newspapers in my district, but to a personal mailing list as well. (At that time there were not more than a dozen members of either branch following that procedure. At present, I would guess that more than half do so.) When I moved over to the Senate in 1954, I continued the "Reports," but with one change; instead of sending them each week, I sent them every other week. This was partly because the pressure on my time was greater in the Senate and partly because the Senate moves more slowly.

Other members, in both branches, have since developed and enlarged upon the idea. Some have made their newsletters into pictorial pamphlets. (Usually the members sending them have figured largely in the pictures!) I never adopted that method. Those picture spreads are probably legitimate, and they can be attractive and interesting; but it has always seemed to me that they are a little too obviously political propaganda. My "Reports" were brief and were confined to a discussion of what I considered the most important measures before the Senate at the time, how I voted on them, and why. They stimulated a good many replies from the recipients, which, whether favorable or unfavorable, helped make the "Reports" productive and worthwhile.

In this regard there is one marked difference between the practice followed in the House and in the Senate. The House has always voted itself the privilege of sending out literature addressed only to "Resident" or "Boxholder." The Senate, on the other hand, does not permit this. Consequently, each senator must acquire a mailing list, which over the years can entail substantial personal expense. I have believed, however, that it was money well spent, because it is much more personal and thus more effective to have Mr. and Mrs. John Jones, living at 15 Kimball Street, receive a letter or report with their proper address and their names spelled correctly.

Other expediencies are resorted to for building up a closer relationship with constituents. One of them is the questionnaire. Many members of both houses of Congress periodically send out communications polling opinions on a whole series of public issues. I myself never did this, and for two reasons: first, it seemed to me that if you request the opinion of a constituent on a given subject and later vote the other way you are asking for trouble; second, there is a dangerous tendency to slant the questions. For instance, in connection with the latter point, here are three questions on foreign aid: (A) "Do you believe in our extending foreign aid to all or nearly all foreign nations?" (B) "Are you against extending any foreign aid at all?" (C) "Do you believe that foreign aid should be carefully allocated to friendly and under-developed nations who need it and where it will improve the foreign relations of the United States?" These are what I mean by slanted questions: they rather suggest the answers, so that very few people would fail to say "no" to the first two and "yes" to the third. I must add, however, that my long-time colleague, Congressman James Cleveland of New Hampshire's Second District, is one of several who have used the questionnaire quite effectively; and I have noted that he tries to avoid slanting his questions.

Really, however, I do not like the idea of a senator making decisions on the basis of a poll of his constituents or the number of letters he has received from them for or against any given issue. Rather, I would have him conduct his own study, use his best judgment, and then report his actions fully and faithfully to those he represents.

Next, let me consider the other side of the dual role that every senator must play. While it is true that he must not, as I have suggested, become so obsessed with being a national figure that he neglects his own people, it is equally true that he is a senator of the United States and that it is his duty to legislate for the whole country and, as far as it lies in his power, to make his influence felt in the councils of the nation. As his experience and seniority increase, he may well become a real factor in national affairs—even if his name is not emblazoned in headlines or despite the fact that his picture never adorns the front cover of *Time* or *Newsweek*. But, ironically, the man in the street usually wants his senator to be a "big-name" senator—although that same man in the street would be the first to chastise him if, in gallivanting around the country, he were to slight his duties to *him*.

Just how does one become a "big-name" senator? Occasionally, of course, a person of truly transcendent talents enters the Senate—someone who by sheer ability and genius attains national eminence there, if in fact he has not done so prior to his coming. But such people appear only once or twice in a generation. The Thomas Edisons and the financial wizards and, in general, the great thinkers and doers of this world are usually far too immersed in their own "thing" to engage in the rough and tumble of politics. From time to time someone comes to the Senate with nationwide fame already established by, say, deeds of valor in peace or war. John Glenn, the astronaut, as well as military heroes of the past, qualify in this respect. But usually it requires careful cultivation to enable a U.S. senator to become a national figure. Frequently it involves a decision made at the very beginning of one's senatorial service. (We all remember the contrasting definitions of a specialist and a general practitioner: the specialist learns more and more about less and less until he knows everything about nothing; the generalist, on the other hand, comes to know less and less about more and more until he knows nothing about everything.) Sometimes a person entering either branch of the Congress will choose to devote himself to a particular field (such as labor, foreign relations, agriculture, education) or to a particular cause (such as that of the veterans or the elderly or the handicapped), more or less to the exclusion of everything else. He may, in doing so, get himself known as something of an expert in his field, travel about lecturing on the subject, and eventually be invited to participate in television panels and discussions. But in doing this, such an individual often sacrifices, to a considerable extent, the opportunity to acquire an overall knowledge of the Congress and its ways or to gain a breadth of understanding, through associations with other members well versed in various fields.

Someone who does not ride a hobbyhorse or attempt to push himself to the front too soon and who tries to see the forest, rather than the trees, may develop into a very useful and effective senator. However, because of his early reticence and caution, he can get himself catalogued as nondescript or run-of-the-mill, and in many cases such labels stick.

There are certain and definite ways by which a member can make himself a "big-name" senator. Those who happen to be wealthy or have access to ample financial backing may retain the services of the best and most expert public relations firms—sometimes (as in the case of the Kennedys, for example) in both Washington and New York. These professionals seize upon any casual utterance the senator may make—or if he fails to make one, they may do it for him!—and with skillfully prepared news releases, magazine articles, and other propaganda, they broadcast it nationwide. Naturally, these publicity firms have a working relationship with the news media, including nationally syndicated commentators and newscasters. The average garden-variety senator, though he may be hard working and have membership on important committees, is soon eclipsed by this kind of promotional activity. In fact, he would almost have to drop dead on the floor of the Senate to get a national headline!

Once in a while there is a senator who, although he is unable to buy publicity, knows how to ingratiate himself with members of the press and networks. He is adept at dealing with them. (Perhaps he has been a member of the news media himself.) He knows when to wine them and dine them or how to get them invited to parties or to take trips with traveling committees. I am not suggesting that members of the press are so easily bought, but this kind of attention does help.

A third method of getting one's name before the public is by becoming a "maverick" and by attacking the projects of other senators—

or the senators themselves. Frequently, senators of this type attack the procedure of their own party leadership. That is a sure way to grab headlines and get one's name well known. The late Wayne Morse of Oregon was a prime example of those who have resorted to such tactics—a man who once revealed to a group of us in the cloakroom the whole underlying theory of this method, when he laughingly remarked that one of his loftiest ambitions was to throw an egg into an electric fan! This is a sure way of becoming a "big-name" senator, but it does not enhance one's popularity with other members nor one's effectiveness within the Senate. Senators will continue to treat such a person with courtesy and will not in any way seek to ostracize him, but the time always comes when the gentleman wants something for the people of his state, either from a committee or from the Senate as a whole, and he may then receive very little cooperation.

The poorest possible test for measuring the influence and effectiveness of a senator is to base one's analysis on how often his voice is heard. Anyone versed in the ways of the Senate will testify to that. For instance, each day in the Senate, there is what is called a "morning hour," devoted to limited speeches on any subject a senator may wish to discuss. (Senator George Aiken, with his dry Vermont humor, used to say that this was followed by a "eulogy hour," followed by a "righteous indignation hour," followed by an "alibi hour.") Accordingly, there is ample and easy opportunity for any senator to "log" an endless surge of oratory, if so disposed.

The foregoing dissertation on methods by which senators may become well known might, of course, be taken as merely an alibi for those of us whose names have not become nationwide household words. Well, maybe it is!

CHAPTER

IX

Looking Beneath the Surface

It is easier for eight or nine elderly men to feel their
way towards unanimity, if they are not compelled to
conduct their converging manoeuvres under the micro-
scopes and telescopes of the Press, but are permitted to
shuffle about a little in slippers.

—*Herbert Albert Laurens Fisher*

ONE of the fascinating books that I read in my youth was *Life on the
Mississippi*, written by Samuel Clemens under his pseudonym, Mark
Twain. The author was himself a licensed river pilot, although I doubt
that he worked at it very long. But he was a master of words, and the
word pictures he drew of the lurking snags, the changing channels,
and the hidden undercurrents left a lasting impression.

The inner workings of Congress are not always visible to the casual visitor, who is often troubled by what he sees; and through the
years of my service I was constantly receiving letters from home folks
who had enjoyed the many attractions of Washington but were be-
wildered and disappointed by their visits to the galleries of the Senate.
If they visited the Senate on a routine day their disappointment at the
spectacle is easily understandable—a senator droning through a speech
to an almost empty chamber; another senator sitting in the presiding
officer's chair signing his mail. Visitors wonder where their own senators are and whether they are neglecting their duties. Those who have
had this experience are entitled to an explanation, and this seems an
appropriate place for it.

As indicated in previous chapters, debate in the Senate is to an extent unlimited, and it frequently consumes days at a time. Accordingly, the Senate does not sit constantly in serried ranks, any more than an army is always on dress parade. You do not judge a military installation by the number of men who happen to be on guard duty, you know the rest of the personnel are broken up into working details or on the target range or engaged in a score of other pursuits. In the same way your senators, when not in the Senate chamber, are grinding out legislation in their committees, dealing with departmental work for their constituents, or handling mail and other duties in their offices. First and always, the most important job is to study the questions shortly to be voted upon. One hour spent in studying the committee report on a particular bill currently before the Senate, reviewing the evidence and setting forth all sides of the question, provides more basic information than could be gleaned from sitting all day listening to repetitive speeches. After debate has run its course and the voting starts, you will find the Senate in full attendance.

Another point that sticks in the craw of many is the public's impression that the Senate works under a rigid system of seniority. Folks feel that committee appointments and chairmanships should be given on the basis of ability and not on just how long a man has been in office. There is some justification for such a feeling. In the past, it has been true that occasionally a brilliant legislator never reached the top because somebody with sound health and a safe constituency was ahead of him. It has been also true that seniority often hinges on a trifle. (Because I was elected to fill a vacancy and was sworn in a little over a month before the arrival of a new crop of senators, I found myself, at the beginning, outranking fourteen senators, and I retained that advantage throughout the whole twenty years of my Senate service.)

However, during the past decade the rules of seniority in the Senate, and I believe in the House as well, have been considerably relaxed. In less important matters, such as the assignment of offices and seats, there has been no change, for these relate to fixed rules of the Senate which apply to all senators of both parties. The more vital question which has occasioned controversy throughout the years is committee assignments. Here there has never been a universal Senate rule. Each political party is allowed its proportion of committee assignments, as determined by the party in control of the Senate, and it divides them up among its members in accordance with its own rules.

In honesty, I must confess that in this matter, as in some others, the Democrats have been more progressive and less bound by tradition than the Republicans. When I first came to the Senate, both parties were following strict seniority in making assignments to committees, which meant that every freshman senator found himself on minor committees, and it might be some years before he could hope to attain membership on the majors. I must further confess that the Democrats of the Senate have proved to be, in certain practical ways, generally more skillful politicians than have the leaders of my own party. Their leadership realized that unless a new senator was given at least one reasonably important committee assignment, his opportunity for active participation in the work of the Senate during his first term would be lessened and his campaign for reelection made more difficult. As a result, the Democratic caucus, or "Conference" as it is called in the Senate, took the first major step in modifying the rigid rules of seniority, by providing that newcomers would be given one minor and one reasonably major committee assignment, the latter relinquished to them by senior members.

The Republicans do have sense enough to follow a good example set by the Democrats (in those rare cases when they provide us with one), and our Conference, in turn, worked out a gradual and rather elaborate modification of the seniority rule. First, we designated four so-called "blue ribbon" committees—namely, Appropriations, Foreign Relations, Finance, and Armed Services—and provided that in the future no Republican senator could be a member of more than one. (I believe that a fifth committee has since been added to this exclusive group: the Committee on the Budget.) Our Conference went on to define the standing committees that would be considered "major" (beyond those above named) and those that should be rated as "minor." We then specified that no senator could serve on more than two major standing committees, and if he were on two, no matter what his seniority he would not be eligible for membership on any of the special committees of the Senate or joint committees of the Senate and House. These actions opened up a substantial number of committee assignments to freshmen Republican senators that had previously been denied them.

Two final steps were taken during the last years of my service, when I was chairman of the Republican Conference. It was discovered that a few members with much seniority were serving as top-ranking minorty members of two, three, and sometimes even more committees; and we compelled each of them to relinquish all but one of their ranking positions. As a final step in modifying seniority, we provided that at the opening of each Congress, the Republican members of each committee might elect the person who would be their ranking member —or should the Republicans be in control, the chairman—and that the senator chosen need not necessarily be senior in service. (It should be borne in mind that under the rules of the Senate, the chairman of each committee must be ratified by the whole Senate, so that the election by members of the committee could be overruled.) I have gone into perhaps tedious detail on this subject, but it may lay to rest some public apprehension that the Senate has refused to eliminate possible unfairness in its ancient seniority rules.

The effect of these changes has been to prevent veteran senators from accumulating, as in the past, a disproportionate number of powerful committee assignments—so many, in fact, that they could not possibly give the necessary attention to all of them—while, at the same time, depriving able senators, coming up the line, from increasing their opportunity for service.

I recall vividly and with some amusement certain comments made in a meeting of the Republican Conference in the early sixties, when the movement for the revision of seniority rules was in its infancy. I cannot be sure, but I think they were observations made by Senator Jim Pearson of Kansas, who has a rather whimsical sense of humor. He reported that he had just moved to a more desirable office on the second floor of the Senate Office Building. He then remarked that under the senatorial caste system known as "seniority," a member starts

at the top of the office building and moves down, even as he starts at
the bottom of his committee and moves up. "Likewise," he continued,
"he usually starts with an inside office, and it may be several years
before he gets one with an outside view." In the councils of the Senate, on the other hand, he starts on the outside and moves inward. If
he stays in the Senate long enough, he may hope for one of the beautiful outside offices on the first floor, and to be on the inside whenever
policy is being made. "The trouble is," he added, "he is then so old
and decrepit that he can barely totter into his beautiful office and so
deaf that he can't even hear the strategy developed in the councils of
the party."

I had and still have reservations concerning the final step of reform: allowing committee members to elect their senior ranking member regardless of the length of time he has served on the committee.
My objection is that it virtually destroys the last vestige of the seniority system. In going to that extreme, we forget that there is a very
practical reason why the seniority rule should not be completely abandoned. Let me relate an anecdote that will help make my point. The
story involves a visiting student who voiced objections to this long-
standing system within the Senate. The senator with whom he was
talking asked him, "If you and I came to a door together, would you
try to crowd through in front of me?" The student replied, "Of course
not. I'd let you go first." "Then," said the senator, "you believe in
seniority, at least to the extent of avoiding physical complications in a
doorway."

The traditional seniority rule in the Senate had, admittedly, become so rigid and inflexible that it permitted a small group of seniors
to dominate practically all the positions of real influence. Year by year
the autocratic few had become more and more entrenched in their
power. It was high time that the caste system of seniority be relaxed
and the supremacy of the few over the many be eliminated. However,
the seniority system, when not abused, served a real purpose—well il-
lustrated by the above anecdote. Even at its height the seniority system was never able to stifle talent completely. Real ability will always
make itself felt, no matter how far down the table a man sits. And

utterly to disregard seniority and experience, leaving the organization of the Senate and all its committees to the dickering and logrolling of the open caucus, would lead to indescribable confusion and crowding for place.

There is enough crowding as it is. You have heard of the two men lounging on the bank of the Potomac, watching an old rotten log drift by. Said one, "That log reminds me of the government at Washington. There are probably fifty thousand ants on that log, and each one of them thinks he is steering it."

There is another feature of the congressional scene that has become a matter of deep concern. That is the attempted secrecy that has appeared to surround many of the activities of our national legislators, as well as certain of the executive departments. The revelations of Watergate, the heretofore hidden activities of the CIA, and the nature and extent of surveillance of American citizens by the FBI which have come to light since the death of J. Edgar Hoover are all very much in the public eye and are causing widespread apprehension—and properly so.

In fairness, it should be observed that Richard Nixon and his administration cannot be held solely responsible for the concealment of illegal practices which are, manifestly, inconsistent with a free government of a free people. It has been revealed that such secret operations had been going on under a series of presidents. The storm that followed Watergate and President Nixon's attempt to hide certain facts from the American people was the catalyst that focused attention on an ever-widening field of clandestine activities by a supposedly democratic government. I suppose, as the then chairman of the Republican Conference of the Senate and a member of the leadership team that faced agonizing hours contemplating the likelihood that we as senators might be sitting as jurors on the second impeachment of a president in the history of the republic, I could digress here and try to get in my oar about those last harrowing days of the Nixon presidency. However, I am not trying to write a best seller or capitalize on the Nixon tragedy—nor on ghoulish gossip about the private lives and loves of other presidents. Only those outside events that had a definite impact on methods and procedures of the Congress, with particular reference to the Senate, are relevant to my narrative. The whole Nixon-Watergate episode served to bring to a head a long-smoldering complaint that there has been too much secrecy in the workings of Congress.

There has been, as I have acknowledged, justification for this complaint. A prime example is the secrecy that heretofore has surrounded the Central Intelligence Agency (CIA). Every agency of government is supposed to be under the scrutiny of some committee in the Congress—committees known as "oversight committees." Since the creation of the CIA there has been a small, select, joint Senate-House committee to whom that agency has reported and supposedly, in some degree, disclosed its activities. However, that committee, as far as I know, was unique in that the identity of its members was a well-kept secret. Their names did not appear in the *Congressional Record* or the *Congressional Directory*. They never held public hearings, and all their deliberations were in secret. Their identities were not even disclosed to other members of the Senate. Before I retired, I had become one of the most senior members of the Senate, yet I never knew who served on the CIA Committees (although I suspected that the chairman and the ranking minority member on the Appropriations Committee must have been two of them). The allegations that the CIA has been involved in assassination plots abroad undoubtedly will result in some *actual* oversight on the part of Congress.

The excuse always given for all this hush-hush in connection with the CIA has been that if a committee of Congress were entrusted with real information, it might be "leaked" and would endanger the lives and usefulness of our agents in other countries. True, senators and congressmen are by nature talkative, but the fact remains that in the closing years of World War II, the entire Appropriations Committees of the Senate and House were aware of and furnished the money for the "Manhattan Project" (the research enterprise that led to the development of the atom bomb) without once breaking the seal of secrecy.

There is another, more recent demonstration that committees of the Congress (not the whole membership) can be trusted not to divulge classified information. Quite some years ago, a group of senior members of the Armed Services and Appropriations Committees, along with the leadership of both the Senate and House, were summoned to the Pentagon. After being pledged to secrecy, we were told of the development of a new weapon: the neutron bomb. This fearsome device could be dropped from a light plane into any population center of the world, and its explosion, we were told, would hardly be more noticeable than the backfire from the exhaust of an automobile; but within a period of days every human being within a radius of several miles would die, and die horribly. Then, after a few days more, all effects of the bomb would disappear, it was said, with no harm whatsoever to the material riches of the area—banks, art treasures, mints, factories, machinery, fortifications, shops, and homes—undisturbed except by the presence of a city of dead. This horrendous weapon could be produced at comparatively low cost, and we were invited to express our opinions as to whether it should be. I have a vivid recollection that, almost without exception, the members from both houses and both political parties were horrified at the very thought.

Since the days of Attila the Hun, world conquerors have been world robbers, and we were practically unanimous in the belief that to introduce into the world a weapon that would destroy people and leave material wealth intact would be an invitation to conquest and pillage. From that day at the Pentagon, I never heard a whisper about the neutron bomb until, in 1977, President Carter intimated that, to save expense, he was inclined to cancel production of the B-1 manned bomber and to substitute for it the neutron bomb. Apparently his suggestion took the whole country by surprise, for on every hand people began asking about this new weapon. But the neutron bomb was not new; it had been developed more than a decade before. Here, then, is another proof that seasoned members of the Congress can, in fact, maintain security when it is necessary for the public safety. Yet, in the case of the CIA, even the appropriations were camouflaged under various fictitious titles, including "basic research." Thus, the Congress cravenly allowed itself to be excluded from reasonable information that as elected representatives of the nation we should have demanded, and we all must share that guilt.

As far as the CIA and the FBI are concerned, however, the Senate and House will probably be forgiven, for at the worst they can only be charged with being too credulous and trusting. We were not the perpetrators of wrongdoing, but only guilty of a lack of vigilance. The real complaints against us have centered on: first, the little artifices, which have been legislative practice since time immemorial, by which members divest themselves of responsibility for actions that might incur public scorn; second, and the subject of the greater controversy, Congress's refusal to open up to the public and the press the secret, executive sessions of its committees.

There are innumerable examples of the first of these. In May of 1956, for instance, on the eve of an election campaign, the farm bloc was insisting upon a farm bill. The administration and the leadership of both parties, coveting support from the great farm belt, felt bound to provide what was demanded. The bill passed by the Senate was a two-billion-dollar subsidy. It provided for price supports for feed grains, which could have cost New Hampshire dairy and poultry farmers two-and-a-half-million dollars a year, and it projected an export program to dump cotton abroad at a lower price than the costs to textile mills in this country. Moreover, it carried soil-bank payments under which the big ranchers and farmers could collect hundreds of thousands of dollars. All attempts to ameliorate these and other provisions of the bill failed. When at last the time came for the final vote, only four senators, of which I was one, raised their hands to ask for a roll call (it requires ten), so a two-billion-dollar farm bill was passed on merely a voice vote. Here is an inside tip: when an important bill passes without a record vote, you may be pretty sure that everybody wants to say to its beneficiaries, "we passed it," but no one wants to admit "I voted for it." That in itself proves the legislation in question is not a good bill.

One more example. A tax-reform bill was ready for final vote. At that point, the manager of the bill arose and said, "I send to the desk a perfecting amendment." Now, a "perfecting amendment" is assumed by everybody to involve simply the remedying of some technical flaw. The clerk mumbled a few words, and the amendment was accepted. After the bill had passed, it turned out that the amendment increased the tax-free expense allowance for every member of Congress. Such subterfuge is inexcusable. It is encouraging that, in recent years, seasoned and experienced senators are constantly on guard to prevent such trickery. (John Williams of Delaware, one of the most conscientious and vigilant men who ever served in the Senate, speaking in condemnation of these tactics, told of the young farmhand who wanted to borrow a lantern to go courting his girl. The old farmer scoffed at the idea. "I never bothered with a lantern when I went courting," said he. "Yes," said the young man, "but look what you got.")

Now I come to what I regard as the real crux of the present controversy over secrecy in government, at least as far as it affects the Congress: shall all meetings of committees be opened, to permit attendance by the public and the press? For the last few years there has been a constantly swelling tide of sentiment throughout the country that all deliberations by governing bodies be held in public. The reasons for this movement are easy to understand, and they have merit. People are no longer content just to know the public actions and votes of their representative, whether he be in the city hall or in the U.S. Senate. They want to know exactly how and for what he is exerting his influence behind the closed doors of executive sessions. Their mounting demands are a healthful sign and, I hope, indicate the beginning of a reversal of the public's indifferent attitude toward the rights and duties of citizenship. And, in a sense, these critics are shooting at the right target. Just as the workroom of a restaurant is the kitchen, the workroom of the Congress is the committee, and what takes place within its councils is of paramount importance. But the question of opening up all committee procedures is not so uncomplicated as it might at first seem.

It has long been the established policy of the Congress that at the conclusion of public committee hearings on any measure, members of the committee go into executive session to determine what, if any, recommendations the committee will make to the Senate (or House) concerning its disposition. These sessions have been shrouded in all the secrecy of a Masonic lodge. Members were considered on their honor not to disclose what took place therein. A member was at liberty, if he chose, to disclose his own vote in the executive session, on the bill itself or on an amendment thereto, but he was honor-bound not to reveal the vote or position of any other member. In many cases not even members of the committee staff were allowed to remain, they merely held themselves available in case any member of the committee desired to bring one or more of them into the session to answer questions concerning their investigations or to refresh the memories of the committee on some particular point of evidence. To be sure, all this can appear to be a very sinister practice, particularly at a time when the public's confidence has been severely shaken by hidden activities within the executive branch of the government, including federal law-enforcement agencies.

As a matter of fact, even before the public became so sensitive to secrecy in government and during a period when the procedures I have just outlined were the unquestioned practice, it never really afforded much privacy for committee doings. In the first place, its effect was limited to those bills that were buried in committee and were not reported. The instant a bill was reported, the committee had to file a printed report listing the names of all members favorable to and all members opposed to the bill, as well as any who favored the bill with amendments; and the signers of each report usually filed statements setting forth their reasons. So the whole record was there for the world to read. Even in cases where some members of the committee failed to sign the report or to reveal their positions unless and until the bill reached the floor, it did not take long for an alert press, experienced in the ways of Capitol Hill and with "pipelines" reaching into committees and their staffs, to ferret out the position of each senator, once a majority of the committee had formally filed a report. Furthermore, in response to the popular demand for "open" meetings, practically all committees have amended their rules so that every roll call in executive session (whether on the bill or any amendment thereto) is immediately announced to the press by the chairman. That would seem to have broken down the last vestige of secrecy. But, the demand that the press and the public be present and witness the proceedings of all committee meetings still persists.

In light of my own experience, I cannot help but feel that these last demands are unwise and unreasonable. Most crusaders who begin by striving for a thoroughly worthy goal become so dedicated that they go to extremes. In the interests of good legislation, it would seem necessary that at some point members of the committee, having heard the testimony, should have the opportunity in private to take their hair down and discuss fully and freely every aspect of the problem, to exchange their views frankly, to approve those provisions the majority believe to be sound, to reject any that could be harmful, and to be able to alter and amend freely, without having remarks made in an informal discussion magnified or misinterpreted. This would seem true whether it involves a city council or a committee of the U. S. Senate. When we begin having the press and the public present during all deliberations, two results follow immediately: either committee members will meet secretly the night before, thrash out their differences, and come into the session with a carefully rehearsed discussion; or members will fail to appear at the sessions and will simply file their voting proxies with the chairman. That does not lead to careful legislating.

Two concrete examples should make this point clear. On one occasion, the Committee on Commerce was considering a consumer bill providing for what is called "class action." At issue was the situation in which a defect is found in some appliances that had been purchased for less than five dollars and where the individual purchaser cannot obtain voluntary reimbursement from the retailer, distributor, or manufacturer; under such circumstances, obviously the purchaser could not afford to bring a suit at law for such a trivial sum. The bill, therefore, provided that any number of purchasers of such an appliance who desired to do so could join together, employ one attorney, and bring a joint suit. A member of our committee, well known to be a liberal Democrat and a staunch supporter of nearly all consumer legislation, said in the course of our general discussion, "Aren't we inviting jackleg lawyers to go about soliciting clients and building up litigation? Is there some safeguard we can put in this bill so that it will not bring about that result?" Every member of the committee knew he was for the bill and was simply raising an honest objection to one of its features and seeking to improve the proposed law. Yet, the following day the largest newspaper in his home city proclaimed that he was opposed to the bill and implied he was no friend of the consumer. The result was that this senator did not attend another "open" executive session of that committee for many months. Rather than run the risk of misinterpretation, he voted by proxy, thus depriving us of his expertise acquired by long hours on the committee.

As my other example, I would refer to a hearing held by a House committee on appropriating money for a proposed memorial to former President Eisenhower, to be erected in the city of Washington. Mrs. Eisenhower and her granddaughter-in-law, Julie Nixon Eisenhower, attended the hearing and expressed their appreciation that the committee was considering the matter. Then, when the hearing ended, the chairman immediately called the committee into executive session, but announced that it was to be an "open" meeting. Mrs. Eisenhower and her granddaughter-in-law, I am sure with no wrong intent, remained while the committee discussed the amount involved and voted. I doubt if there would have been any opposition to the bill in any case, but it certainly would have been very embarrassing for a member to have raised objections to the memorial with members of the family present.

It would seem fairly evident, therefore, that the adoption of a universal rule that all executive sessions of committees be open to the public and the press could be more harmful than beneficial. Committees may now, if they choose, vote to admit the public to their executive sessions, and they frequently do so. Some measures, somewhat technical in nature, are little understood by the general public, and the public could benefit greatly by witnessing the deliberations of an experienced committee as it goes through the process of refinement and clarification in preparing such a bill to be reported. In many cases deliberations may be made public without in any way stifling free and full debate on controversial points. But in the case of every proposed measure that contains complicated and highly controversial provisions, at some point opportunity should be afforded members of the committee to voice their opinions freely to each other, while searching for some common ground for compromise and agreement. Otherwise, a legislative committee cannot function effectively. Certainly there are aspects of secrecy in our government that call for correction, but the suppression of full and free discussion within the legislative branch is not an appropriate remedy.

Actually, the gravest abuse of secrecy is the tendency of the executive department to mark as "classified" every document its officials can lay their hands on—seemingly, so they can be sure of hiding their own mistakes. In connection with classified papers, there is a story of the bishop who employed a secretary who had previously worked at the Pentagon. Having occasion to look at his files one day, the bishop was astounded to note that they were all marked "Sacred" or "Top Sacred."

In this chapter I have tried to touch on topics about which I have received many questions from my New Hampshire constituents and others. These questions have reflected not so much a real and definite suspicion, as a vague feeling that the Senate sometimes is loath to disclose all the facts to the folks at home. The empty Senate chamber, the seniority system, and closed committee sessions are some of the subjects that have stirred apprehension. There is one other.

A myth seems to have grown up in the minds of our people that the Senate is some kind of a secret society in which members protect each other. The Senate is *not* a club. It is a parliamentary body of individuals representing constituents. Each senator needs the good will of the rest, but only insofar as it can be gained by courteous and considerate treatment. Without the good will of my colleagues, particularly those on my own committees, I would have found it more difficult to help locate an Air Traffic Control Center at Nashua and a Cold Regions Research and Engineering Laboratory at Hanover or to stop a dam at Livermore Falls or to fight the closing of the Portsmouth Navy Yard or to obtain migrant pickers for our apple growers or to have done many other errands of varying importance— all of them necessary for my state. If that makes me a member of a club, so be it—but it makes each senatorial constituent a member, too.

When, indeed, someone speaks of the Senate as if it were an exclusive club, I always remember an incident that involved the late Prescott Bush of Connecticut. Senator Bush will ever remain in my memory as the very prototype of a senator—distinguished, honorable, able. He was a kindly man, as many of us who served with him and under him when we were freshman senators have reason to remember. But Senator Bush had an ingrained contempt for cant and hypocrisy, and he was capable of piercing sarcasm. I recall with intense amusement a conversation which I could not help but overhear when we were both meeting with constituents in the Reception Room of the Senate. One of the ladies talking to him said gushingly, "Is it true, Senator Bush, that the Senate is the most exclusive club in the world?" "Well, that could possibly be said," replied the senator gravely. "We all call each other by our first names. We treat each other with scrupulous courtesy. We and our wives occasionally get together socially. But," he added fiercely, "if one of our members stubs his toe, we EAT him." Senator Bush, always the gentleman, immediately smiled and put the lady at her ease, but I am quite sure that she never again had any illusions about the Senate being a club.

CHAPTER

X

The Filibuster

Ignorant people think it's the noise which fighting
cats make that is so aggravating, but it ain't so; it's
the sickening grammar they use.

—*Mark Twain*

IN preceding chapters emphasis has been laid on the changes that
have taken place in the Congress. There is one respect in which Congress has never changed. The first Congress ever to assemble in this
country was the Continental Congress which met in 1774. Before it
ended, John Adams complained: "Congress [is] nibbling and quib-
bling as usual. There is no greater mortification than to sit with . . .
these great wits, these subtle critics, these refined geniuses, these
learned lawyers, these wise statesmen [who] are so fond of showing
their parts and powers, as to make their consultations very tedious."
Obviously, crusty old John was enraged at the constant delays and
bored to death by the pompous and repetitious utterances to which he
had to listen.

For over two hundred years Congress has been afflicted with this
malady, as has every free parliamentary body in history, and it is in-
curable. Congress consists of 535 human beings subject to human
frailties. The chief of these frailties is the tendency to put off difficult
decisions. When Fort Sumter was fired upon and Pearl Harbor was
bombed, the Congress acted promptly; but barring some such crisis,
our national lawmakers are adept at dilatory practices. Constantly they
postpone. Constantly they appoint study groups or special investigating committees "to report next year." They appear to have a talent for

119

taking a simple, straightforward proposition and lousing it up with amendments. This is frequently the case on controversial measures. Our lawmakers are not only human, they are also politicians, so they are doubly loath to move forward and vote a bill up or down; they persist in a struggle to find compromising amendments that will make the legislation palatable for everybody. (Such amendments are usually dropped by the Committees of Conference between the House and Senate. Otherwise, a measure would be so cluttered with complicated and contradictory provisions as to defy interpretation by the courts or administration by the executive.)

These are the reasons, according to my observation, that the Congress fails to function with "all deliberate speed" (to use the rather contradictory phraseology of the Supreme Court), but whatever the reasons, when Congress appears to be spinning its wheels, the public immediately thinks of the word "filibuster."

The filibuster is particularly a Senate disease. On rare occasions, the House has a mild form of it, when action on some measure is stalled by repeated roll calls and delaying amendments; but under the rules of the House there can never be a real talkathon. It is in the Senate that the filibuster breaks out in its most virulent form, and when these attacks come, the Senate suffers and the public protests. To show you how frustrating and painful a filibuster can be, let me cite a brief excerpt from a "Report" which I sent home to New Hampshire on March 10, 1960:

> As I write this Report, continuous round-the-clock debate on civil rights has been going on for five days and nights with nothing accomplished. Not even one of the reams of amendments has been acted on. This is by far the longest filibuster on record. I must wait to give you the final score, so I'll try to give you a picture of the filibuster itself. Here is a typical day.
>
> 11 P.M. Long of Louisiana having spoken ten hours drones on, reading voluminous court decisions. Senators huddle in the back of the Chamber waiting for the end of the speech and the inevitable quorum call which follows, before trying to snatch a few hours sleep.

12:30 A.M. The quorum call starts.

12:51 A.M. A quorum of 51 Senators is finally rounded up, and Sparkman of Alabama launches into a speech. He says he believes in freedom of speech and proceeds to prove it.

1:52 A.M. Another quorum call. Sleepy Senators stagger in to respond to their names and quickly head back for the cots and couches. Dignified Leverett Saltonstall is in Indian moccasins. Many are without ties. The required 51 is not mustered. A roll call follows on sending the Sergeant-at-Arms to bring more in. As it progresses, enough arrived to make the quorum.

4:50 A.M. Sparkman finishes. Another quorum call. Thirty minutes later enough Senators have shuffled in (and out again), and Smathers of Florida undertakes to keep the flood of words rolling on.

6:45 A.M. Smathers quits. Quorum call and roll call to bring in Senators consume 33 minutes. Then Stennis of Mississippi takes over. He says he has never seen "the Senate in better tradition or in better form."

9:30 A.M. Another quorum call. The ball is passed to Talmadge of Georgia, and so on throughout the daylight hours and into another night.

The filibuster is as old as parliaments. They staged one in the Roman Senate against Julius Caesar. Parnell resorted to it in the British House of Commons, holding up business in an attempt to get action on Irish Home Rule. One of the first filibusters in Congress was the fight over locating the temporary capital of the United States—of which Fisher Ames wrote in disgust, "This despicable grogshop contest, whether the taverns of New York or Philadelphia shall get the patronage of Congress. . . ."

Filibustering has come a long way. No longer is it a personal talkathon by one or two members. It is now a highly organized project with one side appearing in shifts to keep the ball rolling, while the other side stations sentry squads for twenty-four-hour vigils, with the remainder of their forces sleeping in cloakrooms and offices, ready to produce a quorum and grant no respite.

The long and historic civil-rights filibuster which occurred during

March, 1960, and to which I have referred above, was in some respects the most dramatic of them all. Even the elements made a backdrop for it: a blanket of snow lay over the Capitol, while passions seethed within. Mechanical equipment began to fail: one of the tram cars to the office building broke down, and the remaining one was barely limping; and at times the electricity went off, so that quorum bells ceased to ring, elevators stalled, and senators, summoned by telephone, struggled up stairs through the darkness to reach the chamber. But the senators, even the aging ones, kept up the pace. The human body is a marvelous mechanism—and the endurance of the human jaw is beyond belief.

But now let me strip away the nonessentials and get down to the bare bones of the question of unlimited debate in the Senate. Forgive me if, in the interest of clarity, I start with some elementary facts that are probably common knowledge. Debate is and always has been un-limited in the Senate, with only one safeguard. Rule Twenty-two provides that if sixteen senators sign and file what is called a "cloture petition," it shall lie on the table over one legislative day and then a roll call upon it shall take place. The cloture petition provides that debate on the question before the Senate shall terminate. If the re-quired number of senators vote for cloture, debate is not brought in-stantly to a close, but each member of the Senate is allowed to speak for only one hour, and that hour is not transferable.

The question that has occasioned long and bitter controversy each time a new Senate convenes and adopts its rules is how many votes must be mustered to invoke cloture and stop debate. Down through the years, a "constitutional two-thirds" has been required. That rule as applied to the present Senate of one hundred would require sixty-seven senators to close off debate, even if a dozen were absent because of illness or other reasons. A few years ago, Rule Twenty-two was relaxed so that two-thirds of the senators present and voting would be necessary (provided there is a quorum). Recently, the rule was further relaxed so that only three-fifths (that is, sixty) of the whole Senate is required. That is the present situation. At the beginning of each new Congress, as we have struggled with Rule Twenty-two, a substantial bloc of senators has always fought stubbornly to permit a mere majority of senators to choke off debate. I voted for the concession that two-thirds of senators present and voting, instead of two-thirds of the entire membership, should suffice to end debate. I could not go along, however, with the three-fifths notion, because I regard it as merely getting the camel's nose further into the tent, making it easier to take the ultimate step of permitting a bare majority to stifle debate. That is a skeleton history of the controversy; now for the arguments.

There is much propaganda to the effect that the Senate, like Gulliver, is tied down hand and foot by its own rules and that many evils have come from the difficulty of limiting debate—a situation that has resulted in the defeat of many meritorious measures, by simply talking them to death. This gospel is usually preached by those devoted to particular causes who want to whip Congress into faster and more feverish action on their pet programs. These crusaders have found ready response from many good people who sincerely believe that you can reform the world, amend human nature, and enforce the Ten Commandments by acts of Congress.

Although the public has been led to believe that filibusters have blocked much vital and necessary legislation, actually the record does not sustain this allegation. The filibuster, while often annoying, is a hobgoblin, more fancied than real. Except in the closing days of a session, when there is always a logjam of legislation that must be disposed of before adjournment and when anything that provokes long controversy is crucial, filibusters rarely succeed in blocking legislation —and even when they occur at the end of a session they merely delay action until the opening of the next session. In all my years in the Senate, I cannot recall a single instance of a bill's being really talked to death and a final vote on its merits by the Senate being, in fact, prevented. For instance, every bill pertaining to civil rights has reached a final vote and been passed.

Indeed, because of the prominence of the recent struggles over civil rights, the public has the impression that prolonged debates are confined to that subject. People forget that from the filibuster on the United States Bank in 1841 (which caused Henry Clay to introduce the first cloture petition) until this past decade, extended and bitter debates have involved many other issues: tariffs, taxes, expenditures, and war. Many of those issues, and particularly long-term spending bills, still involve potential menaces to the republic, and they call for careful consideration. In the House of Representatives, where because of its size debate *must* be limited, I have seen an appropriations bill totaling many billions of dollars and extending over many years, passed with only two hours of discussion permitted. Free speech in the Senate, giving time to search and weigh every expenditure, could one day save the nation from bankruptcy.

These are some of the reasons the Founding Fathers insisted that in the smaller body, the Senate, the rights of minorities should be protected by allowing them full opportunity to present their case to the Senate and to the country—although, as I have pointed out, the Senate rules have always provided a means of finally limiting debate and forcing a vote. Of late, we have been giving much attention to the rights of minorities in this country—as we decidely should. It is just as imperative that the rights of minorities in at least one body of our national congress should receive adequate protection.

Here is an interesting sidelight. Free speech in the Senate has long been regarded as chiefly a protection for the small states. This is true. New Hampshire has two representatives in the House; California has forty-three. Only in the Senate does New Hampshire have an equal voice. However, this is only part—and a small part—of the story. The large and populous states should take heed. Not too long ago, the Internal Revenue Service estimated that seven states were paying one-half of all federal taxes. Those seven states have, of course, only fourteen senators out of the total one hundred. With their constituents having so much at stake, those fourteen senators may one day have desperate need for time to examine items in some colossal appropriations bill, and to fight long and hard to prevent a crushing burden being placed upon their citizens. Reasonable freedom from gag rule makes the U.S. Senate about the last place on earth where minorities cannot be smothered by majorities. The late Eugene Millikin of Colorado, one of the all-time greats in the Senate, said:

If my country were confronted with the choice of surrendering all rights under our Constitution save one, I would unhesitatingly counsel the preservation of the right of free speech. So long as this right remains unimpaired, all other rights, if lost, may be regained.

There are other and more practical, but nonetheless compelling, reasons the modern crop of eager beavers who are so obsessed with the idea of streamlining Senate procedure should stop, look, and listen. They are forever crying that the rules of the Senate slow up legislation. That is a virtue rather than a fault. At the end of my first sixteen years of service in Congress—eight in the House and eight in the Senate—I recall taking time to review the torrent of bills that had been introduced and the number that passed and became law. I found that during the period 126,903 bills had been introduced and that 13,290 became law. It is much easier to write a law into the statute books than it is to take one off, and the rules of the Senate that were designed to ensure careful scrutiny of proposed legislation were formulated by wise and thoughtful men.

Vice President Alben Barkley, the Senate's number-one storyteller, used to talk of the man who was still a bachelor at sixty-five. Someone asked him why he had never married. He replied that he had been attracted to but one woman, and that upon his first look at her he determined she should be his wife. "Why didn't you marry her?" was the inquiry. His answer: "I took a second look." Those Senate rules the "new breed" of senators are so anxious to discard were framed to afford a chance for the taking of that second look.

Many of our presidents have stormed at the Congress because of its failure to act promptly upon the many recommendations of the executive. Many times we in the Congress have ourselves become impatient. Bear in mind, however, that in all free countries deliberation is the nature of the legislative beast. Only a Reichstag dominated by a dictator acts swiftly.

As a boy I was amazed and impressed by a lecture on the internal mechanism of the dairy cow. I thereafter regarded bossy with a new respect, as a complex machine—a milk factory on legs. She has, I learned, four stomachs: one true stomach and three for storage. In one day she can cram 150 pounds of wet grass into her compartments. Then she retires to a shady place, regurgitates it in small amounts, chews it thoughtfully and thoroughly, and digests it in her true stomach. Congress should be blessed with similar equipment.

In the early days of every session, the White House sends up dozens of recommendations, and they are all labeled "urgent." Members of the Senate and House themselves introduce hundreds more. This mass of fodder is assigned to committees which, in turn, parcel it out to subcommittees. During my years on Capitol Hill, I observed repeated attempts by young, enthusiastic members, who had come to Washington with fire in their eyes, to "get things moving." Even with the assistance of experts from the Brookings Institution and from academia all over the country, their attempts to streamline the legislative process have met with determined resistance. The reason for this is that unless legislatures take their own good time, they cease to be deliberative bodies and become mere rubber stamps for the executive. As Justice Jackson said in the "steel case":

> With all its defects, delays and inconveniences, men have discovered no technique for long preserving free government except that the Executive be under law and that the law be made by parliamentary deliberations.

To which Justice Black added:

> The founders of this Nation entrusted the lawmaking power to the Congress alone in both good and bad times. It would do no good to recall the historic events, the fears of power and the hopes for freedom that lay behind their choice.

We are all aware that the Congress has recently fallen alarmingly in public estimation, and I have addressed myself to certain aspects of this in an earlier chapter. A national poll in 1976 showed that for the first time Congress was at the very bottom of the list of social institutions, with respect to public confidence. Only 9 percent of those questioned said they still had confidence in Congress, as against 42 percent ten years before, in 1966. Yet, Americans who so overwhelmingly express their contempt for Congress as an institution (whatever may be their opinions about individual members) would do well to restrain their emotions and to engage in some precision thinking. They might benefit from a refresher course in history. With all their faults, representative legislative bodies are the bastions and the bulwarks of free and orderly government. When parliaments fail, dictators rise or mob rule takes over.

I would be the last to deny that there have been "do-nothing" Congresses—although the famous Eightieth Congress (1947), so branded by Harry Truman, was not one of them. The Eighty-sixth Congress (1959) was perhaps the worst one in my recollection. It almost failed to leave its launching pad; its second stage failed to ignite; and it ended in a fizzle. There have been others nearly as bad, and we who served in them suffered acutely. Nevertheless, even at my advanced age, I would be willing to appear anywhere, on any program, against any antagonist, and undertake to prove that this nation has suffered more from hasty action than it has from delayed legislation. At the same time, in doing so, I would never attempt to deny the frustrations that are bound to beset members of a legislative body in a free country. Many times, like Alice in Wonderland, we are baffled by the wasted time and futile debate:

> "Well, in our country," said Alice, still panting a little, "you'd generally get to somewhere else—if you ran very fast for a long time, as we've been doing."
> "A slow sort of country!" said the queen. "Now, here, you see, it takes all the running you can do to keep in the same place."

CHAPTER

XI

Salaries and Perquisites

Our praises are our wages.
—*William Shakespeare*

ONE issue that cannot be ducked, if one's discussion of the Senate and the Congress as a whole is to be reasonably candid and sincere, is the question of salaries, expense allowances, and perquisites. "Perquisites" is a five-dollar word that can cover a multitude of sins—and it usually does.

When I became a member of the House on January 3, 1947, the yearly salary of senators and representatives was $12,500. They also received an additional tax-exempt amount of $2,500, supposedly an expense allowance to help enable them to maintain themselves and their families away from their homes during the sessions of Congress. There were four other allowances at that time, not large and easily summarized: (1) provision for one round trip each year to Washington, figured at ten cents a mile, (2) a telegraph allowance, (3) a telephone allowance, and (4) an allocation of paper, envelopes, and office supplies. After thirty years I can no longer remember the exact amounts of the last three provisions. I do recall, however, that we rarely used all the telegraph allowance, so that part of it remained in the Treasury; and that we usually exceeded the telephone allowance, paying the balance from our own pockets (it is hard to refuse a collect call from a constituent).

The only abuse which then existed—other than the tax-exempt $2,500, which I think was dead wrong—was connected with the stationery allowance. Most members used only a portion of it, but they were permitted to collect the remainder and put it in their own pockets, provided they paid an income tax on it. I did not have to face this moral issue, because having been, as I have already indicated, one of the first members of Congress to send out regular "Reports" to constituents, I soon began to use up my entire allowance for paper and envelopes early in each year and, after that, I had to purchase a substantial quantity from my own funds. Shortly after I entered the Senate a resolution sponsored by John Williams of Delaware put an end to any senator's withdrawing cash from his stationery allowance. I was a cosponsor of that resolution. (I believe the House still permits the withdrawal of cash.)

Having laid the foundation, I can now outline the subsequent developments and growth in congressional salaries and allowances. The first time I had to vote on a salary increase came early during my first year in the Senate, in March of 1955. As I phrased it in a "Report" to New Hampshire at the time, I stood up, boldly and brazenly, without hesitation, and voted to increase our salaries from $12,500 to $22,500. There was, I believed, ample justification for that vote.

The cost of living, particularly in Washington, had greatly increased every year. So had other salaries throughout the government. Dozens of officials downtown were receiving more than U.S. senators. Administrative assistants of senators were being held back from receiving salaries consistent with other government employees, because they were fast approaching the salary of the senators themselves. But there were even more compelling reasons for voting that increase of 1955. Congress should never become solely a rich man's domain. Of course, no matter what we do, the wealthy in political life will always have an advantage. Campaigns cost money, and many a citizen simply cannot afford to risk his savings and to neglect his business or profession in an attempt to enter Congress. Another factor to consider is that once in office, a senator or representative may, at some point, find himself out in the cold world, middle-aged, and without either business or profession. It would be a sad day for the country if the Congress were to be open only to those who have inherited wealth or who "have made their pile" and reached an age when they can afford to dabble in politics. Congress will not understand or be able to deal with the problems of our people as a whole unless at least some of its members were not born with silver spoons in their mouths. It must continue to include young men who have families to support and children to rear and educate. Although I personally derived some benefit from the increase for which I voted, it was comparatively slight because it put me into a higher tax bracket, and having only one dependent to declare, a substantial part of my additional salary went back to the government. However, there were younger men with large families, most of them serving in the House of Representatives, who needed it and perhaps could not have stayed in Congress without it.

The most important reason for adequate salaries is that members of Congress should be in a position to be independent. They should not be compelled to accept gifts and gratuities of any kind. My observation has been that instances of our national legislators' accepting gifts or gratuities, other than publicly disclosed contributions when they are in a campaign, have been the exception rather than the rule. Nevertheless, some public men have had to accept financial aid from generous and wealthy friends. Even though they may be innocent of any intentional impropriety, this is a bad practice.

> This is the law, and the law shall run till the earth
> in its course is still,
> That he who eateth another's bread shall do that other's
> will.

Your senators and representatives must be responsible only to the people who elected them; they should have adequate compensation so they need not cringe from or cater to anyone.

Still another reason I voted for the 1955 salary increase was that the bill ended the tax-exempt expense allowance. I am convinced the Congress should always meet this issue squarely, vote its members a salary consistent with the importance and responsibilities of their position, and that the people should know exactly what that salary is. So-called "fringe benefits," including special exemptions and travel allowances, are an attempt to "beat the devil around the bush," and the people are not long deceived. Furthermore, senators and representatives should pay income tax on their full salary, like everyone else. In that way young men with children and dependents will receive the exemptions to which they are entitled, and which other citizens receive, and those without them will pay a higher tax, along with the rest of the nation. That was the theory and substance of the salary increase bill of 1955.

The same bill increased salaries of federal judges. This, too, was in the public interest. Judges should be paid enough to attract able and successful lawyers to the bench. If one had a lawsuit that meant everything to him, he would not want it tried before a judge who had never made good as an attorney. He would want only the best.

I have, as I suggest, no regrets or apologies for that particular vote, but I must admit that the early decisions I had to make in the Senate, when I had only been elected for a two-year period, were all sizzlers. The very first vote that I had to cast was on the censure of Wisconsin Senator Joseph McCarthy; the second, on committing ourselves to defend Formosa; and the third, on raising my own pay. I was beginning to think that serving in the Senate was like working in a steel mill; it would be prudent to spit on anything you were about to sit down on— it might be hot.

Unfortunately, the sound theory embodied in the 1955 bill increasing salaries to $22,500 was not to be adhered to. Shortly after its passage a provision permitting members to deduct $3,000 from taxable income to cover their living expenses in Washington was enacted. This did not restore the $2,500 tax-exempt amount which was supplementary salary, pure and simple, but it did in a measure replace it. It also became the practice to increase fringe benefits, by slipping riders onto bills—bills many of which were routine in nature, with titles having no reference to congressional salaries or perquisites. These were passed without roll-call votes, so that members themselves did not know of the new benefits until notified by the Financial Clerk. Somewhere along the line, the long-existing allowance of one trip to Washington each session was discarded, and provision for the actual expense of several round trips for members, as well as some staff, was substituted.

We had always been allowed one office in our home state or district, located in a federal building if one were available (if not, a limited amount was allocated for rental). In a legislative appropriation bill this was increased to three—three in every state for each senator, as well as three in every congressional district. Of course, this required additional allowance to staff these outposts. Naturally, too, the large states were dissatisfied with this arrangement; and I understand that since my retirement a system of allowable square footage proportionate to the population of the states has been substituted. (California senators get 8,000 square feet; New Hampshire senators, 4,800.) Without a computer, I have no idea how many branch offices this system provides. Recently "mobile office vans" are being provided in which staffers, and occasionally the member himself, can travel around the states and districts, parking in the cities and towns, "furnishing service" to constituents.

I hate to be carping and critical of Congress, and especially I regret being at odds with former associates in the Senate; however, to me this whole approach to compensation and allowances seems inexcusable. The law provides that no office furnished by the Congress may be used for campaign purposes. Perhaps none of these branch offices and mobile vans, and the staffs that occupy them during the years between elections, ever in any way relates to political activity in the interests of their senator or congressman. If you believe this, I marvel at—and congratulate you on—your faith in human nature; I sure as hell don't. But even if those who have these facilities strive for purity, these offices and the traveling that is being done are constantly in the sight of the people, and this necessarily constitutes an advantage for the incumbent against any candidate seeking to unseat him. Such an advantage has never before been tolerated or permitted.

Other allowances furnished for all purposes—postage, stationery, supplies, telephone, telegraph, and travel—are currently thrown into a general pot, and the member apparently is permitted to divide up the sum as he sees fit. The travel allowance can now be used, by both members and staff, between points within their home states, as well as between their homes and Washington. (Incidentally, both members and staff have had their trips between home and Washington constantly increased.)

Apparently to salve its conscience, Congress wrote into the latest law a safeguard that is allegedly directed at preventing the use of these added facilities, including the travel vans, for political purposes—a safeguard so ridiculous as to be almost amusing: the added personnel and paraphernalia cannot be used for campaign purposes during the last two months preceding the member's reelection. For example, the mobile vans, after having served as circulating advertisements for a senator for five years and ten months, or for a representative for one year and ten months, must be ditched or garaged and kept out of public view for the eight weeks before the voting takes place. How consoling that must be to a candidate opposing a sitting senator or congressman—a candidate campaigning without a staff, without the use of the frank, without official offices, and without brightly decorated motor vans! Regardless of the justification (or lack of it) for subsequent increases in compensation and for the expansion of perquisites for senators and congressmen, one cannot escape the suspicion that every step that has been taken in recent years, particularly with respect to perquisites, has been designed to entrench more solidly the members of the Senate and House and to make it more difficult for outside candidates to unseat them.

Although this torrent of fringe benefits and salary increases had not even been dreamed of in 1965, enough of these practices had surfaced after March, 1955, when I voted for a salary increase, that when the Senate came to vote on the next salary increase, to $30,000, I was one who voted against it. But it prevailed. That was the last real opportunity we had to vote directly for or against salary raises, because shortly thereafter Congress resorted to two of the worst subterfuges of all. First, it created a commission to establish federal salaries, including that of Congress, and to recommend them to the president who, if he approved, could place the increases in the budget. Thus, unless Congress took overt action to remove the salary raises from the budget, the raises would automatically take place. By this backdoor method, in March, 1969, salaries of senators and representatives were increased from $30,000 to $42,500. Second, in addition to this, Congress created for itself and other federal employees "an automatic cost-of-living increase," so that in October, 1976 (since my retirement) the salary level for members of both houses of Congress increased again, from $42,500 to $44,600; and beginning in February, 1977, still resorting to the ridiculous expedient of having an outside commission bear the onus of all top federal salaries, Congress has been on a wild binge of increased salaries and allowances that has now reached frightening proportions.

Nothing "turns off" reader interest so quickly as quoting statistics. They are boring and hence ineffective, and they will be found in this manuscript only in very small "homeopathic" doses. Nevertheless, one can have no conception of the pass to which we have come because of the "Pontius Pilate" attitude of senators and congressmen in remaining aloof and inactive while someone else lines their pockets with gobs of taxpayers' money without reference to a brief table covering only a few examples:

1977 INCREASES IN CERTAIN FEDERAL SALARIES

Office	Present Salary	Increase	Percentage of Increase
Vice President of the United States	$65,000	$75,000	14.3%
Speaker of the House of Representatives	65,600	75,000	14.3%
President of the Senate, majority and minority leaders of the Senate and House	52,000	65,000	25.0%
SENATORS AND CONGRESSMEN	44,600	57,500	28.9%
Chief Justice, Supreme Court	65,600	75,000	14.3%
Associate Justices, Supreme Court	63,000	72,000	14.3%
All Judges, District Courts	42,000	54,500	29.5%

The above are only seven rather conspicuous examples selected from hundreds of the higher-paid officials of government, both through patronage and those under civil service, whose compensation increases range all the way from 14 percent to nearly 30 percent— cabinet officers, subcabinet officers, and five classes of so-called "higher-level" presidential appointees, as well as the so-called "super grades" under civil service. For instance, the Public Printer, Librarian of Congress, Architect of the Capitol, the deputies of all these, and innumerable court officers down to part-time referees in bankruptcy, all get increases of not less than 25 percent, and in some cases, nearly 30 percent. The total must be, indeed, appalling.

There are a few grains of comfort coming out of this debacle, however. The public has at least awakened to the chicanery that is going on, and the fury aroused has resulted in a frightened and chastened Congress. The first evidence of this is that both houses have adopted resolutions to the effect that in the future no increase in compensation, for the lawmakers at least, can be adopted without a roll-call vote in both houses. This is at least a very real safeguard against further raises of congressional salaries, for had the Senate and the House been compelled to vote on the most recent raise, they never could have mustered a majority that would dare go on record for it. However, it is much like locking the barn door after the horse is stolen. Furthermore, the outside commission on federal salaries has not been abolished, and it may continue to keep up its pressure. Worse than that, there is no guarantee against the continuing swelling of expense allowances, tax-exempt funds, office space, and staffs. My attention has already been called to one instance in which a senator has nearly twenty employees in only one of his home-state offices. In all my years of service, I never had more than that number manning my Washington office and my one New Hampshire office, combined.

Since time immemorial, oldsters have lamented the decadence of each new generation. Perhaps some of my observations on this subject may be discounted. Indeed, someone may pipe up and say, "Mr. Cotton, what did you do to prevent what has been happening?" For that question I have at least one answer: to the last salary raise that took place while I was in the Senate, I offered an amendment that it should not take effect until Congress had balanced the budget and started the government living within its means. Needless to say, I did not secure enough support even to obtain a roll-call vote.

In drawing this chapter toward its close, I have this further observation: the president has been receiving $200,000 a year as salary, upon which he pays an income tax. Cabinet officers have been receiving $60,000 a year, subject to tax. I maintained while I was still in the Senate that Congress should have the sincerity and integrity to abolish their silly commission and automatic cost-of-living raises and to face up to the responsibility of fixing, deliberately and specifically from time to time, the salaries of all federal public servants, including their own. I believed they should, in view of salaries then received by the cabinet and others, vote themselves a salary of $50,000 a year, not the $57,500 which they now receive. That salary should be subject to the same income taxes, with only the same exemptions, which apply to you and me. It is no cure for the advantages incumbent senators and congressmen have voted themselves (in the form of travel allowances, huge staffs, added office space, free WATS telephone lines, and traveling vans) to reach further into the pockets of the taxpayers and "publicly" to finance election compaigns with tax dollars, for both incumbents and challengers. The time has come for senators and representatives to vote themselves adequate salaries, the amount of which the people may know, and cut out nine-tenths of the fringe benefits and all the rest of the hidden gravy.

I might add here that some of the routine expenditures of the Congress that in the past seemed to relate solely to what one might describe as questionable practices with regard to intellectual honesty, rather than finances, have, due to increased costs, reached serious proportions. One of these concerns the *Congressional Record*. Federal law provides that the *Congressional Record* shall be "substantially a verbatim report of proceedings" of both houses. In yesteryears, this provision was adhered to. A member was furnished with a stenographic report of his remarks on the floor, and he had the privilege of correcting grammatical or typographical errors provided he did not change the substance. Occasionally, when two members lost their tempers and indulged in statements that reflection caused them to regret, they could, by mutual agreement, soften their remarks or, if they obtained unanimous consent, remove the whole dialogue from the *Record*. Gradually, custom began to modify this procedure.

The House was the first to relax the standards involved. With over four hundred members, the flow of oratory became burdensome; and by the time I began my service in the House, the pertinent provisions had been so stretched that members could "revise their remarks" by changing much of the subject matter and even by inserting new material. Thus, people who read the *Congressional Record* were not reading what was actually said in debate, but what the member wished he had said when he thought it over afterward. Soon the rule was altered to the point that members were permitted to insert whole speeches into the *Record*, as if they had been uttered on the floor, when actually they were prepared by the member (or one of his speech writers) and merely inserted as if delivered, even on dates when the congressman was not indeed present in the House.

The Senate held out longer than the House. Senators were "permitted to revise and extend" by smoothing up their rhetoric and occasionally inserting an additional explanatory paragraph, but near the close of my service, the Senate, too, let down the bars completely and members were allowed to furnish speeches and have them appear in the *Record* as if delivered on the floor. Needless to say, the *Record* soon began to fatten with reams and reams of oratory, about 70 percent of which was never actually spoken in the Senate.

Worst of all, members in both bodies in recent years have had *carte blanche* authority to "insert in the appendix of the *Record*" letters or speeches of constituents back home that they felt worthy of bringing to the attention of the Congress. That, of course, means that every senator or representative who desires to please and flatter important constituents can place such texts in the appendix, along with a few complimentary introductory remarks. Thus, the *Record* has become replete with speeches delivered by industrialists at chamber of commerce meetings and with eulogies and tributes and suchlike ad infinitum.

The *Congressional Record* is no longer a journal of facts, but of fiction—and not very entrancing fiction at that. The deception and hypocrisy involved in the *Congressional Record* may have its amusing aspects, but it should not be taken lightly. Congressman William Steiger has, for example, emphasized one very serious ramification. Many federal agencies look to congressional debate for guidance in the writing of regulations for congressionally mandated programs, and colloquies between members of the House or Senate, as published in the *Congressional Record*, often are drawn upon for this purpose. Further, indeed, the "congressional intent" as derived from reported debates has frequently been an important factor in interpreting laws, even by the Supreme Court. Accordingly, when an argument which was never uttered on the floor has been printed in the *Record*—an argument affording no opportunity for either comment or rebuttal—legislative intent can become clouded and distorted.

Lastly, the rising cost of printing and, at the end of each year, binding volumes of never-read (and sometimes unreadable) speeches and proceedings is becoming one more serious drain of taxpayers' money. The year before I retired from Congress, the *Record* contained 38,500 pages and cost $8.8 million. I note that in the fiscal year 1976, it had ballooned to 51,000 pages and cost $14.6 million. By a recent estimate, a single page costs $317 to produce (even by using facilities of the Government Printing Office). Ten years ago it was under a hundred dollars. If the expense keeps escalating and nothing is done to reduce the extraneous material members now toss into the *Record*, the cost of printing it could truly become prohibitive.

A considerable number of concerned legislators, led by my friend Senator Howard Cannon of Nevada, chairman of the Joint Committee on Printing, are making earnest attempts to discourage the abuse of the *Congressional Record*. As a first step, they contend that the use of different-sized type for all speeches and statements not actually made on the floor, or even a less-expensive method of having all undelivered remarks preceded and succeeded by brackets or stars, might do much to dampen the ardor of "orators in absentia."

CHAPTER

XII

Seven Presidents

A big man is a big man whether he's a president or a prizefighter.

—John L. Sullivan, greeting Theodore Roosevelt

As a country boy, born and raised on a hillside farm in Warren, New Hampshire, I never set eyes on a president of the United States until I went to Washington to work in 1925. Back in those days it was a custom of presidents, at noon each day, to receive and greet guests of senators and congressmen. (Today, with hordes of people thronging into Washington, scarcely one in a thousand sees the president, even from a distance.) Often it fell my lot to escort New Hampshire friends of Senator Moses to the White House and take them through the Oval Office.

President Coolidge, despite his many virtues, was not a scintillating personality. I am always amused at the memory of seeing him stand with a completely impassive face, giving a quick shake to the hand of each visitor and repeating in a rapid monotone, "Good morning, how are you?" From his lack of emotion, he might have been counting potatoes back in his native Vermont.

During my years in the House and Senate, I served under six presidents; and, naturally, I gathered distinct impressions of them all, including some of their quirks and peculiarities.

When I entered Congress, Harry S. Truman was president. As a freshman congressman, I had little personal contact with him, but I did have ample opportunity to observe him, for he made a practice of coming to Capitol Hill to address the Congress whenever a situation arose that he felt warranted it.

The single occasion when I met with President Truman in the Oval Office at the White House is one I shall long remember. I cannot point to it with pride, but it did have its amusing aspects. This was during the Eightieth Congress when, for two years, the Republicans were strongly in control. The president had submitted his budget, and the Appropriations Committees of the Senate and House had cut many of his proposed items—not substantially but, to the best of my recollection, about 5 to 10 percent. This was a new departure, because previously Congresses had usually increased the budget and had rarely, if ever, reduced a president's recommended figures. President Truman always had a low boiling point, and apparently he was infuriated by this action of the Republican Congress.

Various agencies of the government, either at the president's instigation or because they, too, resented the reductions, proceeded to make the cuts in areas where they would hurt the most. At that time, the Togus Veterans Hospital in Maine was the only hospital in the three northern New England states equipped to care for mental and nervous disorders. It served all of Maine, New Hampshire, and Vermont, and it also carried a considerable case load from eastern Massachusetts. The Veterans Administration announced that Togus would be closed for lack of funds. Promptly—and quite predictably—all hell let loose. Congress was bombarded with demands by veterans, veterans' organizations, and the public to save the mental hospital.

Under the law, Congress could not restore the funds by passing a supplemental appropriation bill, unless the president's Bureau of the Budget sent up a request for the money. President Truman refused to permit the bureau to make this request. As a result, a meeting was held by all members of Congress from the region affected. John McCormack of Massachusetts, the Democratic floor leader of the House, was asked to arrange for all of us to go to the White House, in order to persuade the president to permit us to restore sufficient funds to maintain the Togus hospital. Truman gave us an appointment and down we went. Naturally, McCormack was our spokesman. He was a friend and supporter of the president, and he had indeed tried to prevent the Republican majority from instituting any of the reductions. Being a freshman, I was not then a member of the Appropriations Committee, but I had voted with the majority to sustain the committee's action.

The hour of the appointment found us all assembled in the Oval Office. The president gave us a rather frigid greeting and inquired why we were there. Congressman McCormack explained the situation to him. He stated that the House was not only willing, but anxious, to restore the funds necessary to keep the mental hospital open.

President Truman had a rather high-pitched voice, particularly when he was angry. Having listened coldly to the McCormack plea, he merely replied, "John, this is not my baby." He added, "I requested sufficient funds, but the Congress turned me down. Congress may now stew in its own juice"—or words to that effect.

"But Mr. President," said McCormack, "I am on your side. I led the fight for your full request in all departments, but we were outvoted by the Republicans. They are now repentant and have agreed to restore the veterans' funds. But we shall be powerless to do it unless you permit the Budget Bureau to send up a request."

"But," said the president, "it's not my baby. I did my part and Congress said no. The baby is on your doorstep. If you lose the hospital, let the Congress take the blame."

McCormack pleaded further with the president, as did other members of the delegation—mostly the Democrats (we Republicans sat in humble silence). The president's sole reply: "It's not my baby." That is all he would say during the hour we were with him, and he said it a score of times. Finally, we gave up and left.

It so happened that within a few days the president came up to deliver his message on the State of the Union. This, as everyone knows, is a very formal ceremony, held in the House chamber. The Senate marches in; the Supreme Court is there; the cabinet is there, as are many foreign diplomats. On such occasions, it is customary for the members of the House who have small children to come early and get seats next to the center aisle, holding a child on their laps. When the president has finished his message, he is escorted up the aisle by a committee appointed for that purpose, and every president makes a point of speaking to the children and shaking their hands.

On this particular occasion, one of my colleagues and I were standing at the rear of the House, watching President Truman greet the children. My friend turned and said to me, "I wonder what he is saying to those children." I replied, "I can tell you exactly what he is saying. He is saying, 'It's not my baby.' That's all he ever says!"

I suspect that John McCormack, along with Speaker Sam Rayburn, subsequently waited upon the president privately, because eventually the required request did come to us from the Budget Bureau, and Congress promptly authorized the added money necessary to save the Togus hospital. But I never saw President Truman after this incident that I did not expect him to pipe up and say, "It's not my baby."

Harry Truman was a stubborn man and every inch a fighter. During later years I had a great respect for him. Of the presidents I have known, I think he was the most unspoiled by the glamour of the high office. He left the White House exactly the same Harry Truman who entered it. He was always down-to-earth. Even his language was earthy—often profane. But, if I may be allowed to use the expression, he had guts.

When the much-idolized General MacArthur failed to toe the mark, Truman fired him. His courage in doing so commanded my admiration, even though I agreed with MacArthur's position—fight to win or get out. If someone criticized his daughter's singing, Truman promptly called him an "SOB." When there was a wave of protest against our using the atom bomb, he told the protestors exactly where to get off, saying, "The Japanese, in time of peace, murdered our men at Pearl Harbor. Let them take the consequences." And he ordered the bomb dropped on Hiroshima.

Harry Truman kept on his desk a motto: "The buck stops here." And it did.

When I moved from the House of Representatives to the Senate, in 1954, Dwight Eisenhower had been president for two years. In the interest of candor, I must confess that my experience under President Eisenhower was something of a personal jolt to me. My admiration of and support for him began when, as a member of the House Committee on Appropriations, I was one of a subcommittee sent to Paris to take his testimony as to the financial needs of NATO, of which he was at that time supreme commander. When, later, Henry Cabot Lodge made a canvass of Congress to get members to join in signing a letter requesting General Eisenhower to run for president, he marshalled only sixteen House Republicans, of which I was one, out of over two hundred. (Many others were doubtless favorable, but Senator Robert Taft had a well-organized campaign underway. Furthermore, Eisenhower had refused to run four years earlier, and they feared that he might do so again, leaving them out on a limb.) Along with Governor Sherman Adams of New Hampshire, I had subsequently been a delegate for Eisenhower at the 1952 Republican National Convention.

I came to the Senate, therefore, with great anticipation that I would be on the "inside" with regard to the president. That is characteristic of exuberant freshman senators, who are apt to enter that body with an exaggerated idea of their own importance. It usually does not take long for them to learn the facts of life and to be cut down to size—as was I. Regarding the Eisenhower administration, there were a few facts that I had failed to take into account. Governor Adams had been the president's floor leader at the Republican convention; he was the top manager of the ensuing campaign; and he came with General Ike to the White House as assistant to the president. Also, Styles Bridges of New Hampshire was the senior of all Senate Republicans; he had served as president pro tempore; he was ranking Republican on the Appropriations Committee; thus, he was easily the most influential Republican in the Senate.

At that time, there were forty-eight states, and New Hampshire was one of the smallest. With Adams supreme in the White House and Bridges reigning in the Senate, it just was not in the cards for the president to give ear to anyone else from our small state, much less to a freshman at the very bottom of the ladder in the Senate.

Happily, both Adams and Bridges were my good friends, and any reasonable and legitimate request that I had was taken care of without my attempting to reach the president. So, as a matter of fact, I had less personal contact with Eisenhower than I later had in the case of each of his successors. Indeed, even to the last year of his incumbency, if I happened to be with a group of senators and others greeting him, I had to tell him my name.

Frequently when I am sitting alone in my home in Lebanon, reliving the past, I recall with intense feelings of nostalgia those days when Ike was president and Sherman Adams was his chief of staff. With Adams at the helm, the White House was a different place than it had been before or has been since. This sweeping statement should require little explanation to sons of the Granite State, for we, particularly of the older generation, know Sherm Adams and our appreciation of him and his extraordinary abilities has remained unshakable through the years. I think the greatest reason for our pride in him is the fact that he personifies all the traits of the traditional Yankee—unflinching courage, unflagging industry, dislike of anything that savors of cant or bombast, and above all, terse and candid in expression. These qualities of Adams, and some of his eccentricities, are as plain as daylight to the people of New Hampshire and Vermont, but they sometimes puzzled and baffled those from other sections of the country who had dealings with him in Washington.

I chuckle when I remember what it was like to communicate with Sherman Adams during his White House years—how different from the nature of response (or lack of response) in other times and with other chiefs of staff there. For example, a typical incoming call from the governor might consist in toto of the following (often without being prefaced by any salutation whatever): "S362—see what you can do to push it along." I might have time to respond, "Will do," but many times not, because Governor Adams's sentence would be punctuated at its end by a sharp click, signifying he, having conveyed everything necessary to say, had hung up. Similarly, if one called him, he was equally terse and to the point—providing such nonexpansive replies as merely "Yep, that will be done" or "No, that can't be done," followed, again, by a disconnect noise on the telephone in lieu of any oral farewell. One always knew where one stood with Adams, and there was no being shunted from one official to another or listening to a lot of airy persiflage. The truly big men on Capitol Hill (and there were and are some), when they got used to him, liked that. The stuffed shirts (and there were and are some) did not like it. They were accustomed to being deferred to.

The country was fortunate to have Dwight Eisenhower as president. Because he had been the allied commander in World War II and supreme commander of NATO, his name was as well known on the streets of Baghdad as it was in Washington. As president of this nation he compelled the respect and, in most cases, the good will of every nation in the world.

During his administration not one American boy lost his life on any frozen steppe or in any steaming jungle throughout the world. Our ambassadors were not assassinated, nor were our embassies mobbed. One sharp word from him and the Red Chinese design to move on Taiwan was abandoned. When the Middle East started to erupt in Lebanon, as it has been erupting recently, he sent the Marines in and the guns were silenced. He did not hesitate to sit on any "trigger-happy" militarists in the country, whether in Congress or out, for he knew war and he hated it. In the first years of his term he balanced the budget for the first time in many years, but the momentum of the reckless commitments made by previous presidents and previous Congresses made inroads that were not controllable in the latter years of his administration. With the world again on fire, would that he was with us now.

I shall never forget the inauguration of President John F. Kennedy. An inauguration is always an enormous, exhilarating national

cocktail: a jigger of pageantry—a splash of military music—a dash
of vaudeville—a jolt of lowbrow political gin—a fillip of high-society
whipped cream. And that year it was served up "frozen"—in ice,
snow, and sleet—the bitterest day in Washington I can remember.

All inaugurals are thrilling because they are part and parcel of
America—Pennsylvania Avenue and Podunk. There are marching
thousands, armored might, governors and other dignitaries; but there
are also small boys darting across the street, despite the frowns of
police, and children bundled in snowsuits, clinging to their parents'
hands. There is the inevitable dog trotting along between units and,
at the reviewing stand, wagging his tail at a grinning president. Such
is America.

And, I must say, from the standpoint of oratory, John Kennedy's
inaugural address was the best I have ever heard. Brief (actually
shorter than Cardinal Cushing's prayer), sparkling, thrilling—delivered with all the power of a young man breathing energy and determination from every pore:

> Let every nation know . . . that we shall pay any price, bear any
> burden, meet any hardship, support any friend, oppose any foe to
> assure the survival . . . of liberty. . . .
> The trumpet summons us again—not as a call to bear arms,
> though arms we need—not as a call to battle, though embattled we
> are—but a call to bear the burden of a long twilight struggle, year
> in and year out. . . .
> And so, my fellow Americans: Ask not what your country can
> do for you—ask what you can do for your country.

The speech was a trumpet call to struggle and sacrifice. However, the same young president in the same speech also promised the
people a considerable number of "goodies," and listening to him I
was reminded of my boyhood days and of my grandfather saying
grace at table, while I waited impatiently to pass my plate. Sometimes I passed it so quickly that I got my knuckles rapped. I won-
dered if the new president was prepared to rap a few knuckles, or
whether everyone would get everything he wanted. Tragically, Ken-

nedy did not live long enough to have that question fully answered.

John Kennedy and I were sworn in as freshman congressmen the same day. We moved over to the Senate at nearly the same time and started our service on the same committee. Of our many contacts one incident stands out in my memory, largely because of our recent problems concerning the importation of foreign oil.

All the senators from the six New England states were, at that time, accustomed to meeting on every other Wednesday morning to discuss problems common to New England, upon which we could unite. Through the years, New England has been penalized by the limitation on the amount of foreign oil it could import, and New England's representatives were constantly pressing each administration to raise the limit on crude oil which could be brought in from Venezuela. But the domestic oil companies were always too strong for us, and each succeeding administration compelled us to pay the higher price required to transport domestic oil all the way from the Gulf of Mexico. Shortly after I entered the Senate, the New England senators (perhaps with tongue in cheek) voted to send Jack Kennedy and me, the two most junior senators, to interview Gordon Gray, chairman of the War Mobilization Board, which was then still controlling oil imports, under the war powers which had been granted by Congress to the president. Down we went, and we met with a stinging rebuff. Gray informed us that the policy of the Eisenhower administration was definitely against any increase of imported oil. I recall riding up Pennsylvania Avenue in a taxi with Jack and how he cussed all the way back to the Capitol, damning the policy which forced New England to pay more than any other section of the country for oil to heat its homes and schools and to turn the wheels of many of its industries.

Less than three years later Kennedy himself was in the White House, and the War Mobilization Board had been terminated. As it happened, I was again one of a delegation to present New England's case for foreign oil importation, this time directly to the president. Jack Kennedy received us cordially, but said that, to his regret, he must refuse our request. I could not resist reminding him of his remarks when he and I had been pleading the very same cause. He smiled and said, "I meant everything I said, but I was then just representing New England, and now as president I have to think of it from the standpoint of the whole country."

Incidentally, I might add that early in Nixon's administration the entire New England delegation went to see him on the same subject, with the same result. The oil companies had not lost their grip. When I think of the dollars and jobs that could have been saved for New England and the domestic oil reserve that could have been created for this country had we been able to import more oil during those many years that elapsed before the Arabic nations, with South America following their lead, put on the squeeze, I am tempted to use some of the same words that young Senator John Kennedy used on our ride up Pennsylvania Avenue many years ago.

In the comparatively short period of Kennedy's presidency, he did not again emphasize, nor did the American people follow, in any perceptible degree, his clarion call, "Ask not what your country can do for you—ask what you can do for your country." But he had a gift for leadership and, I believe, the capacity to become a great president had he been spared. I remember him as a charming and likable young man who worked hard and played hard. Unquestionably he shared, along with the rest of mankind, a reasonable amount of human frailty, but in my opinion the rumors of his immoral conduct after he became president, now being circulated and even printed, are shameful and unwarranted. Guilty of occasional indiscretions, perhaps, but it is absurd to believe that one bearing the onerous burdens of the presidency and being under the microscopic eye with which Washington always observes presidents could have been habitually engaged in sexual misconduct, including wild parties in the White House itself. To come up with new smears on a president years after his death is bad enough, but anything that degrades the presidency reflects upon the nation itself, at home and abroad, and unless completely substantiated is unforgivable.

Lyndon Johnson was the fourth president under whom I served. He was the first president whom I could really call a warm personal friend. He was a member of the House of Representatives when I entered it, but he quickly departed to the Senate. In the Senate, I served under him during the many years he was majority leader and also during the briefer period that he presided as vice president. When he became president in 1963, I had attained sufficient seniority in the Senate and on its committees so that I saw much of him in his years in the White House. I cannot speak with authority about all the leaders of our nation during our two hundred years of history, because I have not been around quite that long. But I would venture a guess that Lyndon Johnson was the most complex and amazing personality who ever served in American public life. He was not necessarily greater or more effective than other leaders that I have known, but he was certainly different.

He was dramatic in whatever role he played. This was his nature, and he could not help it anymore than he could control the color of his eyes. Had he been a man of lesser intellect and abilities, he might have been called flamboyant. None of us who were his colleagues will ever forget his dynamic personality, so clearly displayed in the place where he was at his best: the Senate. We remember how he used to persuade and cajole us, as he moved about the floor, putting his hand on our shoulders, straightening our ties, while he confided to us what he was seeking to accomplish and why he needed our help. We remember him, equally well, in moments of deep tension, when he stirred the Senate with his eloquence—and sometimes even stormed at us. He was a man of many moods: passionate, forceful, harsh, humorous, sympathetic, and kind. But in the end, he was our friend in those days of intimate association.

Physically, Johnson was an impressive, powerful man. His mind matched his body. He was also determined, and intolerant of opposition. Yet, he had some appealing, almost boyish traits. As president, he had full opportunity to satisfy his flair for the dramatic. He signed the Federal Education Bill at the country school he attended as a child. He swore in the postmaster general at the little post office where he mailed his first letter. He signed the Immigration Bill at the Statue of Liberty. In those dark winter days when the casualty lists came pouring in from Vietnam, I almost expected that he would don buff and blue, go up to Valley Forge, kneel in the snow where Washington was supposed to have knelt, and pray for the Congress. He should have; heaven knows we needed it!

Beneath it all, Lyndon Johnson was a wily and adroit politician. He could move men about as one moves pieces on a chessboard. As leader of the Senate he knew exactly when he could apply the whip and the spur and when he should coax with a carrot. When a long, controversial measure with many amendments was before the Senate, he would let the debate go unrestrained for three or four days, or even a week and a half. In such cases, although fifteen or twenty amendments were disposed of in a day, when the Senate came in the next morning there would be twenty-five new ones on the desk. Then, one morning, perhaps a Wednesday or Thursday, he would announce that the Senate must dispose of all amendments and vote on the final passage of the bill that day, even if it remained in session until three or four o'clock in the morning. There would be some squawks, but he always had his cohorts organized and ready to quell any insurrection. So much for the spur. As midnight approached, you could see him buttonholing members who had amendments, getting them to withdraw or to agree to having only five minutes of debate—two and a half minutes on each side. In another hour or two, the Senate would be ready for the final vote, and he would then smilingly hold out the carrot, announcing that after the final roll call there would be no more record votes until the following Monday or Tuesday. And every member of the Senate had been fully aware that that was exactly what he would do!

But even a genius at cultivating good will is bound to come a cropper once in awhile, and Lyndon Johnson made one slip that has caused me infinite amusement even to this day. As a result of the off-year election of 1958 (the year President Eisenhower proclaimed publicly that he could not possibly care less who was elected to Congress, that he could work as well with Democrats as with Republicans), a whole bevy of new Democrats was swept into the Senate: Randolph and Byrd of West Virginia, Cannon of Nevada, Hart of Michigan, Hartke of Indiana, McGee of Wyoming, Moss of Utah, Muskie of Maine, and Harrison of New Jersey. Several of these were assigned to my Committee on Commerce, where the Republican mortality had been heavy. One day I found myself sitting in a subcommittee with four of them, and I happened to notice that they all were wearing large silver cuff links bearing the seal of the Senate. I remarked to Moss that these cuff links were interesting and attractive. He replied that Senator Johnson, on a recent trip to Mexico (where silver is plentiful and comparatively inexpensive), had procured a supply of them inscribed with the Senate seal and had presented a pair to each of the new senators. Shortly thereafter, I began to notice similar cuff links being worn by a considerable number of senators on both sides of the aisle. Then, one day I happened to be in an elevator with Lyndon, who said, "Norris, I have been looking for you. Come into my office for a minute." He opened a drawer in his desk and took out a small cardboard package. Then, rather impressively, he said, "Norris, when I was in Mexico recently, I had some cuff links made to give to a few personal friends in the Senate. I consider you one of my particular friends, and this is the first opportunity I have had to present them to you." I expressed my thanks and said that coming from him, I would certainly cherish them.

About three weeks later, during which I continued to observe most of the Senate wearing these same cuff links, the majority floor leader and I found ourselves leaving the Senate together as it adjourned. He grabbed me by the shoulder and said, "Norris, I have been looking for you. Come into my office." Whereupon he took me into his office, opened his desk, took out the familiar package, and with the same remarks he had made on the previous occasion, presented me with a second pair of cuff links. Obviously, he had passed out so many that he could not remember who had received them and who had not!

I must hasten to add that although this amusing incident might seem to smack of insincerity, Lyndon was not insincere. Lyndon Johnson loved the Senate and had a soft spot in his heart for every one of his colleagues. As proof of this, he would not go into any state and actively campaign for candidates who were running against any sitting senator with whom he had served, including Republicans. This is a policy he followed as leader of the Senate, as vice president, and as president; and no persuasion from the Democratic National Committee or anybody else would move him. This was a peculiar principle, and I never knew of any other senator who shared it; but it was his code of conduct, and he adhered to it steadfastly. It is small wonder that he exerted so much influence with all his colleagues.

As president, Johnson gave more attention to cultivating the Congress than did any other chief executive I have known. He was usually as astute in his methods as when he had been floor leader— but not always. His first message on the State of the Union was a masterpiece. With billions required to continue the war in Vietnam and billions more to carry out the flowing promises of the "Great Society," many had thought he was hopelessly impaled on the horns of that old dilemma, guns or butter—that if he cut back the expand- ing welfare programs to support war, the liberal left would rise up in wrath; that if he chose butter and welfare instead of guns, the conservative right would be after him with terrible swift swords. But he outfoxed them all by an adroit combination of diversion, delay, and reverse field running. He appeased the right by reaffirming his intent to stand fast in Vietnam. He charmed the left by insisting on the last full measure of the "Great Society." And he diverted and delighted congressmen with the lure of a four-year term. He left his listeners so dazzled by his matchless legerdemain that they half be- lieved we could have all the guns we needed, all the butter we wanted, and still come out whole.

As members recovered from the spell cast by that initial message, behind-the-scenes talk centered on how many of his recommenda- tions the president really wanted and how many were made tongue in cheek, expecting Congress to pare them down. Certainly he could not have wanted all the provisions for which he asked, and no one believed he could do all those things—least of all the president, who had served on the Appropriations Committee himself.

Underneath all his skill and power, Lyndon Johnson was an ex-

tremely sensitive individual. He could not bear to leave criticism un-
answered. One day, regrettably, I lost my temper on the Senate floor
and charged him with failing to keep a promise he had made to me.
It was a trivial matter. Debate on an amendment had been limited
by vote, so many minutes on each side. I had asked for five minutes,
and he agreed that I should have them. Obviously, he had uninten-
tionally promised too many senators too many minutes. Time ran out,
and I could not secure recognition. Such things happen constantly,
and it would all have been forgotten the next day or perhaps the
next hour; but, characteristically, he seized me by the arm and led
me into his office, saying, "Norris, I know you want to be fair, and
I want you to understand what happened." I replied, "Forget it, Lyndon. I'm sorry I flared up and will take my remarks out of the record." But he was not satisfied. He hung onto my sleeve and insisted
that I say to him that I would have done the same thing in his place.
And, of course, I said it.

With his kind of sensitivity, I am sure the storm of criticism over
Vietnam, referred to in the press as "Johnson's War," cut him to the
quick, and firmed up his resolution not to run for a second term. I
fear that he retired a bruised and unhappy man, and that brooding
over his loss of popularity and its effect on his place in history led
him to an early death. But he never lost the affection of those of us
who served with him and under him in the Senate—who loved him,
even *for* his faults, which were very human faults.

Lyndon Johnson was not the only president who left that high
office filled with frustrations, bitterness, and grief. There must have
been many throughout our history. Franklin Pierce, New Hampshire's only president (who bore the blame for bleeding Kansas and
was not forgiven, even by his neighbors and former friends in Concord and Hillsboro), undoubtedly was one. And the most conspicuous one who relinquished the highest office in the world, disgraced
and heartbroken, was the fifth president under whom I served, Richard M. Nixon. I shall not even attempt to try to analyze and discuss
the Nixon case. Whole books have been written about it, and many
more will come in the future. Richard Nixon was and is my friend.

We were sworn in the same day as freshman congressmen. We were both members of the now fairly well-known Chowder and Marching Club, a group of fifteen young Republican congressmen who, through the years, met weekly in each other's offices to discuss legislation, politics, and other matters of mutual interest. In the Senate I served with him when he was, first, a senator and, then, vice president of the United States. I campaigned for him in the ill-fated presidential campaign of 1960, when he lost to John F. Kennedy. At least three times—twice as vice president and once thereafter—he came to New Hampshire at my request and spoke at statewide Republican gatherings. On two occasions he spoke on my behalf when I was running for reelection.

After he became president, I became chairman of the Republican Conference in the Senate and, accordingly, I was one of the five Republican leaders who went to the White House regularly to meet with the president. In that capacity I went through those harrowing hours and days that led to his resignation and departure. With others who had been his friends through the years, I went at his invitation to the Cabinet Room the last night he was in the White House, when he desired to bid us farewell, and I saw him break down in tears at the end. That night, at two o'clock in the morning, he called me at my apartment, as doubtless he did other of his long-time associates, for a personal goodbye. He was then in command of himself, and the conversation was extremely personal—to be remembered, but not repeated.

Briefly, may I comment. Richard Nixon and Lyndon Johnson had one thing in common. Both had devoted their whole lives to politics. Johnson's LBJ Ranch and Nixon's New York law practice were purely incidental. Johnson was liked; Nixon was disliked. Nixon had transcendent abilities, but he lacked warmth of personality. The liberals hated him because he defeated Helen Gahagan Douglas for the Senate in a bitter, ruthless campaign. The columnists and TV commentators had no use for him.

Whatever Nixon was, he was not an idiot. Therefore, he could not conceivably have had any advance knowledge of the Watergate break-in, which was an incredibly foolish undertaking. Obviously, the president learned of it after it happened, and apparently he was terrified at the prospect of what the news media would do to him and to his presidency, for which he had fought so long and against such odds, should it become evident he was involved. In his despair, he repeatedly and solemnly assured the American people, for a year and a half after it had been reported in the newspapers, that he had no personal knowledge of the Watergate break. That was untrue, and on that I would not try to defend him. Undoubtedly, President Nixon would have been impeached by the House and probably convicted by the Senate if he had not resigned.

I find that I have been criticized because during all the time of the revelations about Nixon, and since, I have never indicated how I would have voted on impeachment. Friends have told me they were disturbed by my refusal to commit myself, that one reason they had always supported me was that during my years in the House and Senate I had never failed to take a stand on any vital issue and had never hesitated to make my position known. The reason for my silence, however, can be readily understood by anyone who acquaints himself with the law governing the impeachment of a president. The House of Representatives adopts the articles of impeachment, containing the charges of the "high crimes and misdemeanors" that the president is alleged to have committed. The House then appoints a "Board of Managers" to present the evidence before the Senate. The Senate sits as judges—or, perhaps it could be said more accurately, as jurors—to hear the evidence presented in support of the charges and to listen, as well, to the defense presented by the president and/or his counsel. The chief justice of the United States presides. At the end, the Senate votes on whether the president has in fact been guilty of impeachable conduct. As the trial starts, each senator takes a special oath to vote on the guilt or innocence, without prejudice, strictly on the law and the sworn evidence presented. (Even if the special oath were not administered, a senator's oath of office would require such a posture on the part of a member of the Senate.) In view of this, I cannot see how it would be proper for any senator to declare, in advance, for or against impeachment. Many did so; a few others refused, as I did.

Just what an impeachable offense is can be argued by lawyers on both sides. It is already being argued. It seems likely that withholding facts or telling falsehoods while not under oath is not in itself impeachable. If it were, a number of presidents could have been impeached. It seems equally true that if a president conceals or aids in concealing the truth, to the point that he is obstructing justice, that is impeachable. Had the sworn evidence clearly shown that President Nixon was guilty of impeachable conduct, I would have been compelled to vote for his impeachment, painful as it would have been to do so. If, upon the presentation of the evidence in the defense, I had a reasonable doubt, I would have voted for acquittal. I never had to make that decision and never had the opportunity to listen either to formal allegations or to sworn testimony supporting or refuting them, so I cannot know how I would have voted.

Suffice it to say that I am still Dick Nixon's friend and that I grieve for him and for Pat and his daughters. That is all I have to say.

Gerald R. Ford came to the presidency about a year and a half before I retired from the Senate. Although my service with him as president was brief, my association with him had been long and close. He, too, was a freshman congressman with me. He, too, was a member of the Chowder and Marching Club. We were both appointed as members of the much-coveted Appropriations Committee of the House the same day, and we served there together until I moved over to the Senate. Our contacts continued uninterrupted, not only in our weekly conference in the C & M Club, but after, when he became minority leader of the House of Representatives and my seniority had enabled me to become one of the official Republican leadership in the Senate and we were both in the group that regularly conferred with the president. At his invitation I gave a Lincoln Day address in his hometown of Cedar Rapids, Michigan, and at my request he came to New Hampshire, first, as minority leader of the House and, later, as vice president, to address Republican dinners.

Gerald Ford is what the old-time New Hampshire Yankees would

ERRATA   PP. 158 "CEDAR RAPIDS" SHOULD
                          BE "GRAND RAPIDS"

call a "plugger." In other words, he is not a scintillating person. He lacks the capacity to excite or to stir people, but he is cautious, thorough, and a precision thinker who, given time, can be trusted to make sound decisions. There were many who accused him of being inclined to waver and to change his stance on some of his early decisions. It should be borne in mind, however, that for many years Jerry Ford was the leader of his party in the House of Representatives. A floor leader, in either the House or the Senate, is always faced with the problem of uniting his party, as far as possible, on important issues. To persuade nearly two hundred congressmen of varying views, many of them quite individualistic, and to bring about concerted action can only be accomplished by a certain amount of compromising. That was President Ford's constant duty during most of his long service in the Congress, and it was bound to affect his actions during the very early days of his presidency.

I could not endorse in every particular all of Ford's presidential policies. For instance, I felt that, like some of his predecessors, in his anxiety to propitiate the Soviets, so as to obtain reduction in armament agreements, he displayed at times a lack of firmness, which is suicidal in dealing with the Russians. However, it must be remembered that Gerald Ford fought resolutely to stem the tide of public spending, by vetoing bill after bill that would have led us further down the road to bankruptcy, and that he insisted upon an adequate national defense. Above all, let it be remembered (and those of us who knew him through the years can testify to this fact) that he was possessed of an unassailable integrity, which was the prime need when he came to the presidency and which did much to restore the confidence of the American people in their government. In my opinion, he improved each day that he served, and if he had been elected for four years, he would have gone down in history as one of our strong presidents.

History has shown that there has nearly always been a running battle between the White House and the Congress—even when the president and the Congress have been of the same political party, and this has been doubly true when the president belongs to one party and Congress is controlled by the other. As a rule, the Senate has always been more rebellious in its attitude toward presidents than has the House—perhaps because many senators believe that they themselves should be president.

The late Will Rogers summed it all up in his usual humorous fashion:

Distrust of the Senate by Presidents started with Washington, who wanted to have 'em court-martialled. Jefferson proposed life imprisonment for 'em. Old Andy Jackson said, "To hell with 'em" and got his wish. Lincoln said, "The Lord must have hated 'em for he made so few of 'em." Roosevelt whittled a big stick and beat on 'em for six years. Taft just laughed at 'em and grew fat. They drove Wilson to an early grave. Coolidge never let 'em know what he wanted, so they never knew how to vote against him. . . .

CHAPTER

XIII

Senators with Whom I Served

I never considered a difference of opinion in politics, in
religion, in philosophy, as cause for withdrawing from a
friend.

—*Thomas Jefferson*

UNQUESTIONABLY, it is a privilege to be allowed to serve in the U.S.
Senate. It can come to only a comparative few of our millions of citizens, and it is an experience that should be treasured. Of course, persons react differently to life's opportunities. In my case, I never
expected to be a senator, and when I became one I found it hard, at
first, to realize the fact. (I hasten to add, however, that my attitude in
no way resembled that of a colleague who came in during the same
year, and who was inclined to be critical of others. Later, he used to
say that during his first year in the Senate, he spent much of his time
wondering how he got there, but during his second year he began
wondering how the rest of them got there.) Stranger yet are the feelings of one who, having led the crowded and busy life of a senator for
twenty years, finds himself back home, retired. Sometimes I find it
hard to realize that I was ever there.

After all, what can one bring away from the Senate other than the
satisfaction of having rendered some degree of service to one's country, plus some fast-fading memories? In most cases, not much else. In
these days of popular distrust of official Washington, many people
seem to assume that everyone who has served in the Senate has, to
some extent, "feathered his own nest." To be sure, there are a few who

161

do. For example, I recall with amusement a senator who was so solidly entrenched in his own state that his continued reelections were assured. Yet, he always saw to it that some easy pushover would file against him, so that he could hold fund-raising dinners and organize financial committees to raise a substantial campaign fund, most of which remained in his own pocket. The instances of such practices, however, are few, and they came abruptly to an end when Senator Dodd of Connecticut was censured by the Senate, and thereafter defeated for reelection because of allegations by the Senate Ethics Committee that he raised large sums for his campaign and then used them for his own purposes.

In the main, the trophies that come to us, whether from groups in Washington or ones back home in our states, are limited in number and only of sentimental value: a few scrolls, plaques, and bowls of silver or pewter, inscribed with sentiments of appreciation. These we admire and cherish, but we ask ourselves if that is all we have to show for long years of public service. A few months out of Washington and the answer comes to us. The greatest and most enduring reward for all our endeavors is the friendships and associations we had through the years with members of the Senate of the United States.

Some were seniors when we entered the Senate, and we felt the impact of their personalities and the inspiration of their friendship for only a few years, and then they were gone. Others came in with us or shortly thereafter, and we grew gray along with them, side by side, as the years passed. Still others came as youngsters when we, in our turn, were soon to leave the scene, and we witnessed their youthful exuberance with amazement, shaking our heads mournfully as we secretly lamented, "the Senate is going to pot." (Of course, it did not occur to us that our seniors had regarded us with the same dismay fifteen or twenty years prior.) I am convinced that the memories of senators with whom I served are the richest heritage I have from my days in the Senate. Let me mention only a few of those with outstanding personalities, and if, to make them more real, I occasionally mention their idiosyncrasies, it is not in disparagement.

When I entered the Senate in 1954, there were a few veteran

giants still there who soon departed, either by death or retirement: Richard Russell of Georgia, the senior Harry Byrd of Virginia, Eugene Millikin of Colorado, and last but not least, New Hampshire's own Styles Bridges, who, having entered the Senate at an unusually early age, was then the senior in service of the Republican members.

Richard Russell was for years the acknowledged leader of the "southern bloc." Indeed, at one Democratic National Convention the delegates from the South insisted on voting for him for the presidential nomination through many ballots. He himself, however, never showed any interest in the presidency—which proved his worth, for it has been my observation that in most cases a senator, once he catches the presidential bug, ceases to be worth a "tinker's damn" as a senator. Russell perhaps had the most thorough knowledge of the Senate rules, including the precedents that interpret them, of any man who ever sat in the Senate. He engaged in debate only on rare occasions. When he did so, he spoke quietly, but a silence fell upon the Senate and every member listened attentively, which is about the highest tribute a senator can receive.

Senator Russell's convictions were fixed and firm. For instance, it has become a custom for senators to join as cosponsors of a bill, particularly if it has an appealing title indicating that it contains some benefits for veterans, the elderly, or other worthy groups or causes. Through such cosponsorship, senators can "make time" with their constituents, claiming coauthorship. Senator Russell frowned upon this custom and steadfastly refused to join as cosponsor of any measure prepared by someone else. He gave me a sermon on this subject when I was a freshman, and I followed his advice to the extent of always refusing to become a cosponsor of a bill unless I had some part in its preparation and definitely knew what was in it. How could the Senate give careful and impartial consideration to a bill if more than a majority of the senators had declared themselves for it in advance, because of its attractive title, without knowing what was in it? (Fortunately, many senators, learning of dangerous provisions in a bill, will vote against it—even though their names appear as cosponsors.)

Midway in my service in the Senate, Senator Russell developed inoperable, terminal cancer. It was indeed tragic to watch him, day by day, as his strength failed and as his slackening powers forced him, gradually, to lay his burden down. But even then, in spite of his weakness, we would occasionally see a flash of that intellect that had been one of our mainstays for so many years.

When Richard Russell was near death at the Bethesda Naval Hospital he sent his proxy up to the Senate, to be used in the close contest between Byrd of West Virginia and Ted Kennedy of Massachusetts, who were competing for the post of assistant floor leader of the Democrats. Just before the vote was taken in the Democratic caucus, the secretary of the Senate telephoned the hospital and learned that Senator Russell was still breathing, so his proxy was counted. Within the following hour he passed away. Thus, he had performed his duties as a senator from Georgia to the very end.

Senator Harry Byrd of Virginia was another unconquerable warrior. One of his principal missions in life was to keep government efficient, effective, and reasonably compassionate—without permitting it to exceed its proper bounds and to become burdensome to the people. He pursued that objective as governor of Virginia and through long years of service in the Senate of the United States. To the last day of his long life, he held Virginia in a close grip. He exercised control through what was called the "Byrd Machine," but it was not a machine in the sense that word is customarily used. It was not run for profit or for power, but only to attain the goals to which Harry Byrd had dedicated his life, and to organize all Virginians who shared his convictions.

For a time I served on the Finance Committee, of which he was chairman. He was a lovable, friendly man, but he ruled his committee with a rod of iron. The Finance Committee deals with tax legislation. When former Governor Francis P. Murphy of New Hampshire passed away, it was discovered that the last revision of federal inheritance taxes which repealed the former system had, apparently through an oversight, failed to be retroactive to the date when the former tax had expired. Governor Murphy's decease took place during the few months that constituted a hiatus in which neither law applied and, as a consequence, his estate suffered. My old friend and schoolmate at Exeter, Robert Hamblett of Nashua, was handling the Francis P. Murphy estate, and he asked me to introduce a bill to remedy this technical defect. I did so and approached Harry Byrd to ask for a hearing.

He greeted me cordially, even affectionately, for I was one of the stalwart band of senators who voted with him, constantly, against what we thought were unnecessary expenditures. He had a habit of slapping a friend on the back and laughing, as if they were both enjoying a good joke. I asked him for the hearing. He continued to pat me on the shoulder and to laugh, but he said, "Sorry, boy, you can't have a hearing on it. This committee hasn't time to act on every minor flaw in the tax laws. We're constantly engaged in major revisions." I then asked if he could not assign a couple of members of the committee as a subcommittee, just to hear the story. He said, "This committee never acts through subcommittees, but only as a whole." "But," said I, "it's embarrassing for me to notify a leading lawyer in New Hampshire, who is settling the estate of a former governor, that I can't get him even a hearing before a commitee of which I am a member." He continued to pat my shoulder and laugh. "Sorry, boy, if we gave you a hearing, we would be holding hearings every day on tax complaints." Then, with a final hearty laugh and a slap on the back, he ushered me out.

Not long afterward I left the Finance Committee—not because my back was sore, but because after the death of Senator Bridges I was eligible for appointment to the Appropriations Committee, which I greatly preferred. When Senator Byrd retired shortly before his death, his seat was taken by his son, the present Harry Byrd, who carries on the family tradition.

One of the keenest minds, as well as one of the sharpest tongues, in the Senate was possessed by Eugene Millikin of Colorado. Whenever he engaged in clashes on the Senate floor, he was adroit and deadly. I only saw him in the last months of his career. Crippled and deformed by arthritis, he suffered constant agony and had to be wheeled into the Senate. Nonetheless, even under these circumstances, he could still put to flight almost any senator who dared to match wits with him in debate.

One of Millikin's favorite victims was Senator Paul Douglas of Illinois, who had for years been a professor of economics, starting, I believe, at Amherst College and winding up at the University of Chicago. Douglas was able and sincere, but sensitive and excitable, and he found it hard to keep his cool when baited. As a senator, he was an extreme liberal and favored federal financing of many attractive social programs. Earlier, however, during his academic career Douglas had written a textbook on economics, in which he laid down many rather severe principles not consistent with his subsequent liberal philosophy. Millikin kept a copy of the Douglas textbook in his Senate desk, with many of its salient points carefully underlined. Whenever Douglas took the floor to advocate some of what Millikin considered hair-brained schemes, Millikin was promptly notified by an assistant whom he had stationed on the floor. He would immediately have himself wheeled to the Senate, where he would take out Douglas's book and, with a pleasant smile and sweet manner, would proceed to demolish many of Douglas's arguments, using quotes from his own textbook—this until he had Douglas perspiring and in a rage. Normally a serious statesman, he was more like a mischievous boy on these occasions, and his tilts with Douglas seemed more effective than codeine to assuage his constant pain.

Styles Bridges was not only the senior of all Republican senators, as I have already noted, but he, in my opinion, exerted more influence on more senators than any other senator I have known. That influence was not confined to his own party, but included a considerable number on the other side of the aisle. The same popularity he enjoyed in the Senate, he enjoyed to an even greater degree in his home state where, I believe, he had the affection and friendship of more individuals than any other senator who ever represented New Hampshire.

His strength in the Senate and at home was not predicated either on excellence as an orator or on skill as a legislator (although he had a remarkably sound judgment in legislative matters). His greatest asset was his personal charm. That charm was based on the fact that he liked people and never tired of meeting them, studying them, and mingling with them. All over the country he knew more people by their first names than any other public man in political history—with the possible exception of Jim Farley. Had Styles Bridges come from a larger state or had he been blessed with more robust health, he could, I believe, have become president of the United States.

Styles remained the senior senator—indeed, very much the senior senator—from New Hampshire until his death in 1961. It was never difficult for me to adhere to my junior role as New Hampshire's "other senator," because he and I had been fast friends from the time we first met, as young men in our twenties. He knew that I was loyal to him and, therefore, he never resented it when I had to vote differently from him. In fact, he once quoted to me words that he attributed to Lyndon Johnson: "When two men always think alike, you may be sure that only one of them is doing the thinking."

I have never witnessed such an outpouring of affection, nor have I ever seen so many senators actually in tears, as when, after Senator Bridges's death, the Senate met to pay its tribute to him. It was a contradiction of the humorous and rather cynical remark once made by Vice President Marshall, to the effect that the number of people who mourned the passing of any politician would depend entirely on one thing: whether it was good weather on the day of the funeral.

Another shrewd and able senior, whose friendship I enjoyed and from whom I learned much, was Bourke Hickenlooper of Iowa. He used to say, rather ruefully, that his peculiar and difficult name had always been both a political asset and a liability. On the debit side, he had an amusing story.

Seventy years ago—and I, too, remember it well—many mothers used to believe the old-wive's tale that a little asafetida placed in a small bag and hung around a child's neck would provide protection against contagious disease. (That could have been partly true, because it smelled so horribly that it kept people at their distance.) Senator Hickenlooper said his mother once asked his father to stop at the village drug store and get a half ounce of asafetida, there then being an epidemic in town. His father complied, and the village pharmacist packaged a half ounce. The senior Hickenlooper's credit was good, so he casually said "charge it." The pharmacist opened up his account book, took his pencil, and started to enter the purchase. An instant later, he threw down the pencil and said, "Take it, with the compliments of the house. I'm not going to write 'Hickenlooper' and 'asafetida' for ten cents!"

Following Bridges in seniority, on the Republican side of the aisle, was Vermont's George Aiken. During my latter years in the Senate, our seats were across from each other, just as our homes were across from one another on the banks of the Connecticut River, which separates Vermont from New Hampshire. Senator Aiken will always live in my mind as an exemplar of the sterling and attractive characteristics of a real Vermonter. He was able and shrewd, very unassuming and down-to-earth. He was quick to detect any pretension or sham on the part of others. He had all the dry wit of his Vermont heritage, and his sotto-voce comments, whispered during the forensic flights of some of our colleagues, not only livened up the long and dreary hours of debate, but they have remained in my memory to this day.

Senator Aiken did me but one disservice. I happen to be cursed with what some people call a "finicky" stomach, something which was discovered by some of my classmates back in college days, who spoiled many a meal for me by voicing their suspicions as to what might be found in the particular food we were eating. One morning Senator Aiken joined me at breakfast, while I was enjoying what was then a favorite of mine, raisin toast. George took one look at the toast and remarked that it reminded him of an old Vermont ditty entitled "Alternating Currant Pie." He recited it:

> Alternating currant pie,
> Just beneath the crust they lie,
> First a currant, then a fly,
> Alternating currant pie.

I didn't finish that raisin toast and have not eaten any since.

Of all the Senate's seniors at the time I entered, the one with the most striking personality was Everett McKinley Dirksen of Illinois. When William Knowland, at that time Republican floor leader, left the Senate to run for governor of California, the Republican minority in the Senate instinctively turned to Dirksen, and he was their unanimous choice for that post. The first word that comes to mind when one thinks of Senator Dirksen is "gifted." He was endowed by nature with more talents than almost any man I have ever known. He was a natural-born orator—eloquent, persuasive, and forceful. He was a specialist in the use of words, with a nearly boundless vocabulary. From boyhood he must have been a tireless student, possessed of an extraordinarily retentive memory. I have never known a man with such a well-stocked, encyclopedic mind. He was literally a compendium of human knowledge.

Senator Dirksen also had an endless fund of stories and anecdotes to embellish his speeches and to illustrate his points. A couple of quick examples: a tearful wife obtained an audience with Dirksen's friend, the governor of Illinois. The purpose was to beg the governor, on behalf of herself and her five small children, to release her husband from prison, where he was serving a sentence for breaking, entering, and theft. She said he was needed at home, and that although he did break into and enter a store, he did not take much—only some petty cash and a couple of hams. "Is he a kind husband and father?" queried the governor. The wife replied that, to the contrary, he was a brutal, cruel, unfeeling husband and father. He beat her frequently and was rarely kind to the children. "If that is the case," said the governor, "why do you want him home?" "Because," she replied, "we're out of ham."

Second: Dirksen frequently compared the present Republican party to a football team at a small Illinois college which had just had a disastrous year. The coach remarked that their greatest ground gain in the entire season was a five-yard loss, and added, "We never won a single game, but we learned a lot!"

I first served with Everett Dirksen in the House of Representatives, where he was one of its most brilliant leaders. I well remember that his insatiable appetite for acquiring facts and details caused him to go

home every night with a briefcase bulging with material. The people
of his district took such pride in his influence and leadership in the
House, and the distinction he brought to them, that they raised a fund
and sent him on a trip around the world. The members of the House
shared his constituents' admiration for him. While he was still a relatively young congressman, he was prevailed upon to let his name be
presented to the Republican National Convention for president. He
had the distinction of being publicly endorsed by every Republican
member of the House. The effort was mounted too early in his career,
and it was doomed to failure because at that time he was not nationally
known. In later years, after he had won national recognition, he could
well have aspired to the presidency, but perhaps for reasons of health
and advancing age he never did so.

Dirksen had many "hobbies" and causes outside the mainstream of
legislation, and for these he struggled ardently. One was his crusade
to make the marigold our national flower. In this he was always
strongly opposed by Senator Margaret Chase Smith of Maine, who
waged an equally aggressive campaign for the rose. One of the touching scenes of my memory was the day when almost the entire Senate,
along with members of the House and many of the president's cabinet,
accompanied Senator Dirksen's body to see it laid to rest in his hometown of Pekin, Illinois. Just before the graveside service began, Margaret Chase Smith approached the coffin and gently laid upon it a
marigold.

Another senior whom I admired in my freshman years was John
McClellan of Arkansas. A stouthearted, natural-born fighter, he was
possessed of deep, unshakable convictions and a powerful voice that
rang through the Senate chamber—and sometimes out through the
corridors of the Capitol. He was chairman of the special Committee
on Crime, and he fought with all his might and main for legislative
restraints on the Supreme Court, then known as the "Warren Court,"
which seemed so anxious to tip over convictions and to free murderers
and rapists—who frequently murdered and raped again. Near the end
of my service, McClellan became the chairman of the Senate Appropriations Committee. When he was in his seventies, a strong faction

in Arkansas, which apparently regarded him as too old-fashioned in his ideas, waged a determined campaign to prevent his reelection. But McClellan, who had the vigor and energy of a man half his years, stumped his state and won reelection.

In contrast to McClellan, his colleague from Arkansas, William Fulbright, a Rhodes Scholar, former president of the University of Arkansas, and the chairman of the powerful Foreign Relations Committee, was the suave intellectual leader of the freewheeling internationalists who dominated that committee. The only time I recall having seen Fulbright ruffled was when a young senator had offered an amendment cutting off all foreign aid to a certain Iron Curtain country. Senator Fulbright, in a fatherly, almost patronizing manner, called the young man's attention to the fact that he had no knowledge of the history of our relations with that particular country, because he had not served on the Foreign Relations Committee. Fulbright then looked over his half-moon glasses at the young senator and said, "I believe I am correct that my young friend is not a member of the Foreign Relations Committee. Is that true?" To which the brash youngster, apparently irritated at being talked down to, replied, "No, I do not serve on the Foreign Relations Committee. In fact, I am not a member of *any* subversive organizations." Fulbright's face flushed a bright red, and he indignantly demanded that the senator retract his remarks, which reflected on a great committee of the Senate. Amid some laughter, the senator retracted his statement.

One of the ablest and hardest working of my seniors was Senator Case of South Dakota. His sudden death from a heart attack, which occurred on the floor of the Senate, was a great loss. Case was a perfectionist who studied every measure, whether it came from his own committee or another, with painstaking care. I am sure that it will not constitute in any sense a reflection upon one of our number whom we greatly respected, and for whom we sorrowed, if I mention a nickname he earned in the Senate. (In doing so, it will serve to illustrate the casual, good-humored banter that senators, like any other group of men, indulge in with their fellows.) In his seeking of perfection, Francis Case was a stickler on punctuation. Many times, after a bill

had passed through intensive study by a committee and during long
days had been considered and amended, hashed and rehashed on the
floor of the Senate, it would be ready for final passage (sometimes late
at night). At this point, with tired senators impatiently awaiting the
final roll call, so they could go home, Francis Case would habitually
rise and offer one more amendment. He would explain that in order
to show the exact intent of the statute, within a certain line of a certain
section the comma should be changed to a semicolon. The result was
inevitable; he was always referred to as "Semicolon Case."

In this same vein, I might mention that sometime after Case left
us Senator Miller of Iowa appeared on the scene. He had, before he
came to the Senate, been a tax lawyer, and a good one. Tax bills are
probably more technical than any other legislation, and Miller eventually became a very useful member of the Ways and Means Committee, which deals with taxes. But long before that, from the first
day he entered the Senate, he studied every line and section of every
tax bill; he was much concerned with any technical deficiency or apparent ambiguity. He even had an attaché of the Senate place a typewriter in the Republican cloakroom, and as any new tax bill was
approaching its passage, one would find him working away, with the
hunt-and-peck system, pounding out clarifying text and technical
changes. Then, just before the bill reached its final passage, he would
appear on the Senate floor with not just one, but sometimes two or
three amendments, which are called "perfecting amendments." You
can imagine that to have these offered in the closing hours before a
final vote—sometimes in the early morning hours after a long day—did
not endear Senator Miller to his colleagues, although he was respected
for his ability and highly regarded. (Twice his typewriter mysteriously
disappeared from the cloakroom, but on each occasion he obtained
another or made use of one in some adjoining office.) Therefore he,
like Case, acquired a nickname which stuck: "Perfecting Amendment
Miller."

Two other southern senators stand out in my memory, not only
because of their personalities, but because each has fulfilled a very
particular mission in the Senate. One of the stalwart figures I have

admired through all my years in the Senate is John Stennis of Mississippi. He is one of the finest gentlemen I have ever been privileged to
know. (Incidentally, I have always said that I have known but two
senators who really looked like senators. One was the handsome,
white-haired John Bricker of Ohio; the other is John Stennis.) Senator
Stennis has rendered valuable service in many fields, but there is one
in which he has for years been the acknowledged leader. As a member, and for many years as chairman, of the Committee on Armed
Services and the Appropriations Subcommittee on Defense, he has
long been the Senate's champion for vigilantly keeping up America's
military, naval, and air strength.

Sometimes in moments of sadness and anxiety there intrudes a little gleam of humor that will cause a smile. It will be recalled that
Senator Stennis was mugged and shot by two of Washington's deni-
zens, as he alighted from his car to enter his home late one afternoon.
Most men would have collapsed and died, but, with his iron will, he
walked into his home and had Mrs. Stennis call an ambulance to take
him to Bethesda Naval Hospital. There he fought for his life, hov-
ering between life and death for many weeks. Every member of the
Senate loved and respected him, including those who had often disagreed with him. We were filled with apprehension and concern,
awaiting each day's bulletins of his condition. Finally, there came a
sad evening when the word was brought to us that he was not expected to live through the night. The next morning when some of us
gathered, as was our custom, for breakfast in the Senate dining room,
the news came that he had not only survived the night, but was showing marked improvement and his doctors were hopeful that he had
passed the crisis and was on the road to recovery. Naturally, we re-
joiced, but with quiet, reverent restraint. Then, suddenly, a young
Senate attaché, who was at table with us, interposed a remark.

It so happened that the second-ranking Democrat on the Armed
Services Committee was Stuart Symington of Missouri. He was an
able and highly respected senator, but he was much more liberal than
Stennis. While he had concern for his nation's defense, he was more
inclined to divert a portion of defense monies to social programs at

ERRATA   PP. 173 "BETHESDA NAVAL" SHOULD
BE "WALTER REED ARMY"

home and abroad. The remark of the young man was: "Don't worry, Senator Stennis is going to recover. He isn't about to turn that committee over to Symington!" In spite of our continuing concern for Stennis, a laugh went around the table. I am sure John Stennis was not at that point thinking about Symington and the committee, but it is true that he fought his way back to recovery, and toward regaining his old vigor, by sheer will power and his determination to live.

The other southerner I would like to mention is Senator James B. Allen of Alabama. A comparatively new member, who entered the Senate in 1969, he almost immediately gravitated into the position of leadership of the southern conservative bloc, held for so many years by the late Richard Russell. There were reasons for this. He not only was experienced in other legislative bodies, but he is endowed with a natural talent for legislative leadership. He had scarcely warmed his seat in the Senate when he had mastered its rules and many of the details of its parliamentary procedure. A tall, powerfully built man, with reddish sandy hair, he is always courteous, always self-controlled; but whenever any radical measure or amendment in the slightest degree violates fundamental freedom, promotes bureaucracy, or saps the treasury, he opposes it with a bulldog tenacity and is able to invoke every expedient of rules and procedures to block its passage or adoption. He is a power for the cause of rational conservatism in the Senate, and the country owes him much.

An able and skillful senator who came in with me was Gordon Allott of Colorado. He was a master of legislative procedure, but he was possessed of an even greater talent—as I discovered when I was reviewing his activities before going to his state to campaign for him in 1966. In dealing with the Pentagon, as well as other departments, he succeeded in maneuvering into his state more military installations and defense industries than were gained by any other state, with the possible exception of California. He was defeated for reelection in 1972, at the very height of his career; and it is interesting to note that he was, in a sense, the author of his own undoing. The industrial activity which he pushed into his state, while it brought employment and prosperity to Colorado, also brought in thousands of new employees, mostly union-oriented, who helped change Colorado from a Republican to a Democrat state; and this drove Allott from the Senate. The same changes contributed to the defeat of his colleague, Peter Dominick, one of the best legal minds in the Senate.

New Hampshire, too, has gained more industry in proportion to its population, in the last few years, than any other New England state and most other states throughout the country. For this we rejoice. But when I look at the influx of labor from Massachusetts and at the mushrooming growth of our southern-border towns, I suspect the political power in New Hampshire is shifting, much as it did in Colorado.

It is hard for me to accept the fact that Roman L. Hruska of Nebraska, who took the oath of office the same day I did (for we both were elected to fill out unexpired terms of deceased senators), has been lost to the Senate by retirement. He was long the ranking Republican on the Judiciary Committee, and he was one of the best lawyers in the Senate. He will be missed.

There are some other interesting colleagues I would like to mention—for instance, the two senators from Hawaii. The junior senator, Dan Inouye, is of Japanese blood, but his Americanism can never be questioned, for he gave his right arm to his country in World War II. He is able and likable, with much personal magnetism. I served with him for years on the Commerce Committee. Patiently he tried to teach us how to pronounce his name correctly. One day an amendment was offered to a bill, and a senator, incensed by it, spoke up sharply: "I will not accept that amendment—*in no way!*" Instantly, Dan Inouye smiled and said, "Gentlemen, that is exactly how you pronounce my name."

The senior senator from Hawaii, Hiram Fong, is of Chinese ancestry. Like many Orientals, he has an impassive face, but behind it lurks an alert mind and a keen sense of humor. On one occasion a group of senators stopped over in London on their way to attend an interparliamentary conference. While they were there a member of Britain's Parliament gave a dinner in their honor. The toastmaster introduced them, one by one, for remarks. When he reached Fong he said, "I am pleased to introduce the next of our guests. He is the first American senator of Chinese ancestry. Unlike many—perhaps most—Americans, he has no English blood. The distinguished senator from Hawaii, Hiram Fong." Fong rose to respond. Solemnly, without a flicker of expression, he said, "I must correct our good host. He said I had no English blood. I must tell him that my great-grandfather ate Captain Cook." That brought down the house.

It seemed that in all my committee assignments, through the years, I was constantly finding myself lined up with (or, if you want to speak in a partisan sense, lined up against) two senators. One was Warren Magnuson of the state of Washington, chairman of the Commerce Committee, on which I became the senior Republican member, and chairman of the Appropriations Subcommittee on Health, Education and Welfare, on which I was, again, his opposite number. The other was John Pastore. I served with Senator Pastore on the Commerce Committee, where he ranked second to the chairman; on the Appropriations Committee, including several of its subcommittes; and on the Joint Committee on Atomic Energy.

I owe much to Warren Magnuson. He was and is one of the most powerful men in the Senate, and one of its best committee chairmen. While he kept his committees firmly in hand, he was always fair and considerate of every member, including those of the minority party. He and I were thrown together constantly, particularly on the Appropriations Subcommittee. The chairman and ranking minority member of each subcommittee are expected by their respective party leadership to be present at all hearings. Health, Education and Welfare encompasses a wide range of activities, and our subcommittee heard literally hundreds of witnesses each year. Consequently, Chairman Magnuson and I sat together through weeks and months of hearings, many times far into the evening, and a majority of the time without any other subcommittee members present. When the hearings were ended, the time would come to "mark up" the bill. Other members would then be in attendance, but Magnuson and I, having heard all the evidence, had the major role in writing the bill and defending it in the Senate. It was a rewarding experience to work with him.

As a U.S. senator, John Pastore will always occupy a unique place in my memory. I shall remember him as one of the most dynamic, forceful, and effective legislators I have known. Rhode Island is the smallest state in the Union—not much larger than one of New Hampshire's counties. In physical stature John Pastore was perhaps the smallest senator. He is always neat, well groomed, and meticulously dressed. Were he a man of lesser intellectual attainments, he might have been called "dapper." But, because of his ability and capacity, not one of his colleagues ever thought of him as small. By virtue of his Latin ancestry he could, on occasion, become quite emotional. He was possessed of a fiery temper, but this he always kept in close restraint. He was a gentleman in the highest tradition of the Senate. There were senators who were sometimes a bit careless about living up to that standard, but they soon learned not to take liberties with John Pastore, for few, if any, could match him in repartee.

One day, when years of friendship and mutual esteem permitted the liberty, I asked Senator Pastore how he had acquired his prowess in debate and why he was frequently so belligerent. His reply was characteristic. With a broad smile he said, "When you are the smallest boy in the school, you learn to run like hell or fight like hell, and I guess I chose the latter."

Senator Pastore could, on occasion, be cuttingly sarcastic. He had a way of riddling the opposition with one sharp sentence. I well remember sitting in the committee room with a few other senators while the staff was telephoning vainly, trying to locate enough other members to make a quorum. It happened to be on Columbus Day, and a couple of our number (I suspect purposely trying to get a rise out of John) began arguing that it was Ericson, not Columbus, who discovered America. They continued to belabor the subject. Hope of obtaining a quorum was fading. Suddenly Pastore picked up his papers and left the room. As he was going out the door he said, "Yes, yes, gentlemen; of course Ericson discovered America. That is why we are meeting today in the District of Ericson."

I dwell a bit on Senator Pastore not just because I like and admire him, but because he has one powerful attribute that in all my years

I rarely knew another senator to possess. Any member of the Senate will tell you that last-minute speeches on the floor do not change votes. At that point, every senator knows exactly how he intends to vote and rarely, if ever, will he change. Yet, I have seen John Pastore do that very thing: cause men, at that juncture, to alter their intent. Not once, but a number of times I have watched him take the floor, usually on some important amendment, and with a few words, going straight to the heart of the issue, actually influence enough votes to determine the outcome. In that respect, one can almost say that he is unique. Senator Pastore has now retired from the Senate, and he will be sadly missed.

I could not possibly conclude this chapter without expressing my appreciation of and admiration for my New Hampshire colleague who served through the last twelve of my years in the Senate, Thomas J. McIntyre. Senators from the same state frequently find it difficult to get on together, because unlike House members, they both serve the same constituency and they are apt to find themselves competing with each other to get the lion's share of credit from the home folks for any benefits that go to their state. Even if the senators themselves try to avoid friction, their overzealous staffs may bring it about. Senator McIntyre is a liberal Democrat; I am a conservative Republican. We were poles apart in our political philosophies, and we rarely voted together; but from the day Tom McIntyre entered the Senate he leaned over backward to cooperate with me for the good of our state and I gladly reciprocated. There was never a rift between us or any fear on either of our parts that the other would ever seek to take any unfair advantage. The fast friendship we formed did much to lighten the load of my last years in Washington, and my deep regard for him will continue to life's end.

CHAPTER

XIV

Ever-Present Issues

Too few have the courage of my convictions.
—*Robert M. Hutchins*

IT IS NOT the purpose of this book to try to sell my own political philosophy. However, it would be impossible for me to paint a picture of Congress without touching on the perpetual issues that have been the main bones of contention in the Congress and in the country ever since the end of World War II. Obviously, I cannot discuss these prime issues with honesty and candor unless I do so from my own viewpoint. Indeed, I feel I would be remiss if I did not stress some of the directions we appear to be taking, and my fears as well as my hopes for our future.

One ever-present and ever-growing problem I am reluctant even to mention. But it cannot be evaded, because the day of reckoning has come. It involves our national solvency. The reason for my reluctance is that there is no more certain way to bore people than to start expatiating on the fiscal condition of the government. Every seasoned political candidate knows this. He has learned that he may dwell upon foreign relations, health, education, and crime. He may even drop a hint about inflation and unemployment. But the moment he mentions debt, deficit spending, or the need of economy, he turns off his listeners instantly and gets the deaf ear.

However, we can no longer ignore the rising debt and falling dollar. In a neighboring state to mine, where judges are elected instead of appointed, a certain judge failed to win reelection, and he was retired to private life. He secured a job as a bank teller. One day a man approached his window to cash a check. The ex-judge asked him for identification. He produced a driver's license and a credit card. "Not sufficient identification," snapped the judge. "Why, judge," said the man, "I've seen you hang a man on less evidence than this." "Perhaps you did," said the judge, "but now I'm dealing out money, and that's important."

It is indeed important. Most folks think of government financing as some mysterious process that takes place in a faraway realm, the rarified atmosphere of which can only be breathed by economists and statisticians. They have no idea that it reaches into the kitchen and onto the dining table of every family, and may determine our standard of living in the years to come. Long years ago, when Britain was starting down the pathway we now appear to be following, Gladstone warned, "Budgets are not mere matters of arithmetic, but in a thousand ways go to the root of prosperity of individuals and the strength of kingdoms."

During World War I, when farm labor was hard to obtain, many college girls volunteered for farm work during their summer vacations. On one occasion, a farmer entered his barn where the girls were engaged in the evening milking. To his amazement he saw one of them, after she had milked the cow, put the animal's nose in the milk pail and try to make it drink its own milk. To his demand for an explanation, she said, "The cow flicked its tail into the milk and dirtied it, so I thought I had better run it through again."

I am not going to run through again the usual tirade about government spending and its effect upon us—and more particularly its effect upon our children and our children's children. I shall only attempt to hit the high spots and emphasize a few cogent facts.

The one phase of public finance we are expected to ignore completely is the national debt. It was not always so. It was formerly a subject of vigilance and concern, even when our indebtedness was microscopic compared with the present day and when the bare interest on it was not eating into the substance of our people.

There is a legend in the Senate regarding one of the early speeches

of Daniel Webster. That was before we had floods of political literature, and one senatorial orator from each political party was selected
to deliver a comprehensive speech prior to each presidential election.
This speech became the principal document distributed in the forth-
coming campaign. Webster was selected to make such a speech on
behalf of the Whig cause. Senators then lived more loosely and imbibed more freely than would be possible now. Accordingly Webster,
after preparing his speech, fortified himself with stimulants to make
its delivery free flowing and eloquent. In the speech he masterfully
reviewed the issues of the day and then, after a stirring peroration, he
sank back into his seat, hot and perspiring, with brandy fumes rising
to his brain. A nearby senator whispered, "Dan'l, you forgot to mention the national debt." Instantly, Webster sprang again to his feet:
"Mr. President, the national debt—the national debt. . . . Oh, to hell
with the national debt. I'll pay it myself." And perhaps he could have
paid the debt we then had!

Our national debt exceeded $650 billion during 1977, and it is
bound to have a whacking increase after President Carter and the
Congress have finished vying with each other in further swelling the
proposed budget for fiscal 1978–79 (which bids fair to be the largest
in our history—greater than any year during World War II when we
were supporting our own and Allied forces that girdled the globe).
Statistics are dull and leave one cold, but this illustration from the Senate Appropriations Committee staff makes me stop, look, and listen.
There are 525,600 minutes in a year. Slightly over one billion minutes
have passed from the birth of Christ to the year 1976. If the United
States had been in existence and started to go into debt when Christ
was born, we would have had to spend $600 more than we took in
each minute during those 1976 years to create the present debt.

But this is not all our indebtedness by any means. Federal agencies
have been given authority to obligate the government for billions more
ahead, to clean our rivers, purify our air, start public works projects,
to provide employment, finance housing, make small-business loans,
make gifts and long-term, low-interest loans to foreign countries. And
the cry now is that we must pledge more billions to end all unemploy-

ment, extend health care for all Americans, and even guarantee a minimum income for all citizens. In addition, there is a whole flock of "contingent liabilities" for which no funds have been obligated but in which we have pledged the credit of the government to guarantee loans made by banks for housing, small businesses, students, and many other things. The proponents of these claim that they will cost the government nothing, because the beneficiaries will pay them—the same promise you get when you sign a note for a friend.

Available space does not permit my relating here the details of perhaps the greatest trap into which the American people have ever been lured: the Social Security system. The bare facts are that the money paid in has been spent, the cupboard is bare, and with the increasing millions each year who will become entitled to what was promised them, it could cost the country $500 billion—half a trillion dollars.

But the impact of our ever-increasing debt load is not reserved for future generations, although their burden will be the heaviest (providing the republic lasts that long). It is not even awaiting the next decade; it is with us right now. I wonder if our people realize that we are paying forty billion dollars a year for interest alone. That is nearly half the cost of our entire national defense and a substantial portion of all that we spend for health, education, and welfare. Forty billion dollars that buys nothing! It does not build one submarine, provide one hospital bed, train one handicapped child, or pay one cent for medical research. It is one of the prime causes of inflation and compels the printing of more dollars. Not long since, we celebrated our country's bicentennial. The story of the founding of the nation has quickened the blood of all Americans, but one phase of those heroic days got the silent treatment. No one seemed to recall that the Continental Congress tried to meet the needs of the struggling patriots by printing more and more money, until it became utterly worthless; and the phrase "not worth a Continental" has been a common term ever since. But we are doing precisely the same thing today. Our dollar, once supreme throughout the world, is now discounted in many foreign countries, and it has lost its buying power at home. The savings of our people are crumbling. The retirement income of the elderly, no matter how prudent and provident they have been through their working years, is wasting away. So, when one tries to warn of the dangers of deficit spending, it can no longer be taken lightly.

Who is to blame for the fiscal mess we are in? Both Congress and the chief executive share in the guilt, but the burden of the blame must be assumed by the people themselves. My files were always fat with letters from well-meaning constituents calling for economy, but—and there is always a but—Congress must not, they said, cut this or that vital program. There seems to be a universal impression that office seekers are too vociferous in promoting their candidacies, but the combined voices of all the politicians in Washington and elsewhere are as a mere whisper compared with the thunderous propaganda put out by the visionaries pointing the way to utopia by means of more federal programs—most of the proponents of such programs being on the government payroll themselves or financed by some foundation. The fallacy of their approach is the ingrained belief that any human ill can be cured by applying gobs of money, just as our grandmothers used to slap a mustard plaster on our chests for any symptom of whatever nature. Unhappily, the bulk of these huge expenditures is eaten up in furnishing personnel to administer them, and only a modicum finally trickles down to the needy, the afflicted, the handicapped, or the untrained who are supposed to benefit from them.

I am constantly reminded of the minister who, back in the days of foreign missions, approached his wealthiest parishioner with an appeal for a contribution. To his horrified dismay, in response this usually generous man handed him a nickel. Before the clergyman had time to recover from his consternation, the parishioner pulled a roll of bills from his pocket and peeled off two twenties, saying, "The nickel is for the poor heathen. Here's forty dollars to get it to them."

During my two decades in the Senate, our debt ceiling was raised twenty-six times. Each time the same tactics were used by the Treasury Department, and whatever administration was in power, to force Congress to do their bidding. They would wait until the treasury was so depleted that, if there were no authorization to borrow more money within a week, current bills could not be met. Then a resolution raising the debt ceiling would be rushed into both houses of Congress. The terrifying word was brought that if the measure were not acted upon before "next Tuesday," the government would default on its payments, including those to millions of persons dependent on government checks, and that panic—or even revolution—must follow.

In my early days, I used to fall for this line. The leadership on both sides always warned new members of the dire consequences that would attend if, even for one day, the government could not meet its obligations. However, during the latter days of my service, I was one of about twenty-five senators who consistently voted against raising the debt ceiling. I recall that the last time I voted no, Senator Robert Griffin, who had recently been made assistant minority leader, came by my desk and mildly inquired, "Wasn't that a rather irresponsible vote you cast, Norris?" I replied that if I had thought it were irresponsible, I would not have cast it. "But," said Bob, "you people who vote no are forcing the rest of us to bear the onus of raising the ceiling to prevent immediate financial collapse. You know what would happen if next week we couldn't pay our bills." I told him promptly and firmly that that was exactly what I wanted to have happen. It is the American people who are insisting on plunging us deeper in debt. They continue to vote for every demagogue who promises them more federal benefits. If one day the veterans did not receive their monthly checks, those on Social Security did not receive theirs, and the states did not receive their federal welfare money, it might be the only possible means of shocking the nation into understanding that there is a bottom to the barrel. I scoffed at the notion that there would be a revolution. I am old enough to recall that dire day when Roosevelt found it necessary to close the banks. There was alarm, but no revolution; and in a few days arrangements were made to reopen them. I have always believed that the "Bank Holiday" was a clever ruse on the part of FDR to wake up the people and ensure the passage of some of his necessary emergency legislation. If Congress once refused to raise the debt ceiling, arrangements would be made (perhaps a temporary power to borrow) so that people would eventually receive their promised benefits, but it might be a way to make them think twice about sending any more spendthrifts to the Senate and the House. Even that might not work, but it is the only expedient I can think of which might help us stem the tide.

Only an American people aroused to their peril can call a halt on a top-heavy government run amuck. It will only be when our people as a whole realize that a sprawling and nearly bankrupt government lacks the means to exercise genuine compassion that we can hope to stop the leaks and start the long, slow road back to strength and solvency. If President Carter can keep his pledge to balance the budget so that, even for one year, we are not paying out more than we are taking in, that could be the turning point, and I shall praise him for it. I fear, however, that his other commitments and the pull of Congress may force him to follow in the footsteps of many of his predecessors, and he will balance the budget by more borrowing. It was Artemus Ward who said, "Let us all be happy, and live within our means, even if we have to borrow the money to do it."

Having discussed the question of national solvency, my next subject, of equal importance, is national defense. Perhaps no other issue that constantly confronts our lawmakers demands calmer and more carefully calculated decisions—or is fraught with greater hazards if mistakes are made. Unfortunately, no other issue is the subject of so much bitter controversy on so many fronts. The Congress, charged with making scores upon scores of decisions vital to the peace, safety, and security of the nation, has to legislate amid the almost deafening din of dispute and while being pulled, hauled, lobbied, and belabored by the White House, the generals and admirals, the veterans' organizations, and the "peaceniks." It was so in the beginning, is now, and perhaps ever shall be.

Formerly Congress was involved in a constant battle between the services, the army and navy insisting on their own air corps and on developing their own weapons. After a bitter fight the air force was created—and we had one more disputant. After another struggle, all the branches were consolidated under the Department of Defense. Everyone breathed a sigh of relief, hoping this consolidation would

result in the establishment of priorities, avoiding duplication of weaponry between the services, and thus produce more defense at less
cost. However, the Defense Department built up a tremendous su-
perstructure of its own, while retaining all the secretaries and assistant secretaries of each branch—resulting in demands for greater pro-
liferation, rather than less (or so it seemed to many of us in the
Congress).

It is inevitable that the costs of building ships, tanks, bombers,
and the whole range of weaponry are constantly rising, along with
everything else. It is likewise inevitable that the wages of the skilled
labor which produces weapons should skyrocket. But out of the Vietnam War came another sweeping addition to the cost of national
defense. During the wave of civilian hostility against that frustrating
conflict, when young men were evading the draft, colleges were terminating ROTC units, and the American competitive spirit seemed
to be disappearing, the Nixon administration decided that unity
might be restored by abolishing the draft and depending upon a
volunteer army. I was one of a small—very small—minority who opposed this from the start. Although I claim no military expertise, I
just cannot bring myself to believe that in today's world, faced as we
are by powerful rivals who use their tremendous manpower without
restraint and with little compensation, we can possibly hold up our
end of the competition by a volunteer army. The cost of maintaining such an army, even at peacetime strength, saps resources that
we need desperately, to keep pace in the realm of weaponry. A private first-class starts at $418 a month (a sergeant at $539), plus uni-
forms, quarters, board, medical and dental care, and the advantages
of the PX and commissary. If he stays in the service his pay, of
course, increases, and after twenty years (when he is still in his
prime) he can retire, receiving for life approximately half of his
highest compensation, together with many of the perquisites just
mentioned—and be free to engage in any gainful occupation that he
chooses. Civilian personnel of the military establishment, including
everybody from cooks to bottle washers, have approximately the same
pay and benefits.

One has only to turn on the television to hear the many other inducements offered to obtain enough personnel to keep the army, navy, and air force at peacetime strength. With that drain upon our resources, we could go bankrupt trying to compete with our totalitarian rivals, who can draft unlimited manpower at minimum pay. Obviously, armed forces must be led by professional, career officers. However, young Americans subject to a draft fairly administered, with only the obligation to serve two years at an age between high school and college, and with reasonable GI benefits for their subsequent education, could go far in filling the peacetime ranks of our forces; and the money saved could make all the difference in our keeping abreast of our rivals' production of the newest weapons.

In my final years in the Senate, as a member of the two most important appropriations subcommittees—one on defense; the other on health, education, and welfare—I got the full impact of the battle that goes on unceasingly between those who demand that we put all our eggs in the military basket, surpassing our rivals on all fronts, and those who go to the other extreme of trusting in future agreements for limiting arms, to permit the diverting of billions from defense to humanitarian purposes. Having listened months on end to the career people responsible for our defense, as well as to those devoted to social programs, I am convinced that if we are to be powerful and compassionate, we must practice more selectivity in our spending for both defense and domestic programs. Certainly we must not permit ourselves to become a second-rate power, but that does not mean we must excel our rivals in every phase of military might.

Our defense must be based on the assumption that our country will never be the aggressor in a nuclear war. Our need, therefore, is the capacity to survive a nuclear attack and to deliver devastating retaliation, and that capacity must be apparent to our rivals. Thus, our safety does not lie in land-based intercontinental missiles, which can be located and knocked out. Nor does our safety lie in costly supercarriers, which are sitting ducks for the first strike. For purposes of conventional warfare, the smaller carrier—the World War II type, now in mothballs—is still practical. On the other hand, it is suicidal to allow ourselves to be surpassed by the Soviet submarine fleet. An abundance of both attack and Poseidon missile submarines, well MIRVed, is essential. Unlike a supercarrier, a submarine does not have to be attended by a flotilla of ships on the surface and attack submarines beneath. It is a bit of almost indestructible America, roaming the seven seas, and even under the Polar ice cap, capable of wholesale retaliation—even against large land masses like Russia and China. A reasonable number of other weapons, naval and military, are of course necessary, but air power and submarines are the backbone of American defense. Under no circumstances should we bargain away our right to develop them.

That more practical economy in our defense establishment is needed, there can be no question. I always think of the first time members of our Appropriations Committee were taken to the Pentagon for lunch and for a conference with the secretary. They sent automobiles to Capitol Hill for us, and as we rode into the basement of the building, we saw rank on rank of long, sleek, shiny black Cadillacs. I had not supposed there were so many swank automobiles in the world. The sight brought forth sharp criticism from our committee members. The next time they were smart; they sent up a rickety old bus. As we rattled along toward the Potomac, we stared at a sign on the back of the driver's seat which stated, "This bus cost $14,000 and can be quickly converted into an ambulance." And they delivered us at the front door—with no trip into the lower regions, where the sight of luxury vehicles might dazzle the eyes or arouse the ire of simple country senators.

The next vital issue is taxes. They are always with us. ("Death and taxes are inevitable—but death, at least, doesn't become worse each time Congress meets.") Taxation is far too complex a subject to be encompassed in a few paragraphs. Furthermore, I am not a tax expert. However, one cannot serve, after an apprenticeship in a state legislature, thirty years in Congress without having some of the ABCs drummed into him. He may not acquire the high-spun theories of taxation, but he learns a few firm facts, and learns them the hard way.

In my earlier years in Congress, the conservatives—and I suppose I should be counted as one of their number—were forever preaching a "pay-as-you-go" policy: one must not embark on programs unless, concurrently, a tax is provided to support them. The flaw in this theory is that it implies that almost any government activity is justified if you impose a tax to pay for it. My experience, over the years, finally forced me to the bitter conclusion that there is no way on earth to stop the Congress from spending every cent it gets—and then some. (Incidentally, the same is true of every state legislature that I know anything about.) I decided that the only possible way to put some limit on federal spending is to cut federal income, and from that day on I rarely missed an opportunity to vote for any tax cut that was proposed, much to the horror of some of my more conservative friends. Of course, there is a point in the proposition that when you cut taxes, you merely increase government borrowing. But I refuse to believe that that is justification for constantly gouging the taxpayer, particularly the middle-income taxpayer, to feed the insatiable appetite of big government. Besides, there must come a time when an irresponsible government with a devalued dollar will have difficulty in trying to float loans. I believe this country is about to find that out.

That is the first "Cotton maxim." The second is that every tax of any nature is never temporary and is bound to increase. Oh, I suppose there are a few, a very few, war taxes that were discontinued or reduced. Some other taxes were relinquished by the federal government and, then, included in sales taxes by the states. But Congress after Congress in which I served extended most of the many excise taxes that were supposed to be for the duration of the war. And as for the almost inevitable increase of any new tax, one has only to recall the history of the federal income tax and its impact upon our way of life. It was made constitutional by the Sixteenth Amendment and ratified in 1913, just before Woodrow Wilson became president. As a teenager, I vividly recall seeing a list posted in the post office of seven or eight men in our little town who had paid federal income tax. But how much? On incomes up to $20,000 it was 1 percent. Incomes between $20,000 and $50,000 paid an additional 1 percent on the difference, and so on up to $500,000. And no matter how large a person's income, the highest rate on any part of it was 6 percent. No one dreamed that it would ever swell to the point where most citizens pay a third of their entire income to Uncle Sam, and corporations even more.

Nowadays we talk about "big government" and "the huge bureaucracy." All of this came with the opening up of this new and apparently limitless source of revenue for the federal government. Prior to the income tax the government in Washington performed only those functions originally contemplated in the Constitution. With contributions from the states and subdivisions, augmented by tariffs and other income, it maintained our national defense, carried the mails, and dealt with foreign relations. The almost numberless agencies and activities of the government have all arisen since it got its hands on the earnings of Mr. John Q. Citizen.

The federal income tax is perhaps the best example of the maxim that any new source of taxation that is opened up is sure to grow, but it is not the only example, for every state in the Union that has embarked on state income and sales taxes has raised them in almost every session of its legislature. We are reminded of the mushroom, which is famous because once it starts growing it will break through solid concrete surfaces inches thick.

The third "Cotton maxim" is that the worst forms of taxes are the hidden ones. Our huge income tax is a bold and brazen holdup, but at least it is out in the open. But the taxes that rifle purses and empty piggy banks are the excise taxes. Most of them started as war measures and were kept because Uncle Sam, the old spendthrift, must have the money. Webster defines an excise tax as "an internal tax levied upon . . . a commodity . . . an indirect tax that falls on the ultimate consumer." Indirect means "hidden" and ultimate consumer means *you*. Excise tax is a high-sounding name for a sales tax. A sales tax is the meanest tax there is. It cannot hurt the rich. It must hurt the poor. It has all the despicable traits of any sneak thief.

We all remember the analysis of the cost of a loaf of bread; it's old hat now. (In fact, the costs have risen.) It was 2½ cents for the wheat farmer and 24 cents from the consumer—and in between 151 taxes: taxes paid by the baker, the wholesaler, the trucker, the retailer; as well as taxes paid on the salt, the yeast, the shortening, the wrapping.

Some pocket-picking taxes are justified as "luxury" taxes. They are not. The rich man has but one face to shave, just like the poor man. Both pay the same tax on shaving lotion. People with low incomes use the telephone, ride on buses, and need automobiles to go to and from their work. I still believe any American is entitled to a refrigerator, an electric stove, and a television set. These are all honeycombed with taxes.

When I was a boy we used to play "crack the whip." A line of boys ran hand-in-hand, the biggest one at one end, the littlest at the other. Suddenly the big one stopped, and the line snapped like a whiplash. All the boys hung on except the little fellow at the end, who invariably took the tumble. There is your tax picture. The manufacturer, the wholesaler, the transporter, the retailer—and everybody else—pass the taxes along. The consumer, at the end of the line, pays them all.

Even the income tax, despite the high rate paid by corporations, must always be a poor-man's tax. There is a deep-seated notion that big government can be run without touching the little fellow. As one good lady put it to me, "People with incomes under $10,000 should not have to pay any tax at all. Let the rich man pay it." Unfortunately, there are not enough rich men. Tax experts calculate that if Uncle Sam confiscated all individual incomes over $25,000 a year, it would run the government about four days. If he seized all incomes over $10,000 a year, it would support the government less than thirty days. Lincoln said that God must have loved the common people, because he made so many of them. By the same token, you cannot run the government on the rich; there are so few of them. It is that extra dollar or two a week from those who can least afford it that brings in the billions.

There are those in the Congress who want to cut out all exemptions. You have been deducting the interest on your mortgage and on your car payments. That surely is not a rich man's "loophole." I doubt if Nelson Rockefeller or Henry Ford have mortgages on their homes or are buying cars on time. If you practice tithing to your church or contribute to your favorite charity, this sweeping tax reform would hit you. It would also hit your church and your charity. Therefore, be a bit wary in listening to some of this talk about "plugging loopholes." The loopholes they plug may be your own.

Many historians contend that ruthless tax squeezing of the poor and rich alike marked the beginning of England's era of decline. As Sydney Smith put it in 1820, "the dying Englishman, pouring his medicine, which has paid 7 percent, into a spoon that has paid 15 percent, flings himself back upon his chintz bed which has paid 22 percent, and expires in the arms of an apothecary who has paid a license of a hundred pounds for the privilege of putting him to death."

One other question that Congress has been kicking around for nearly two hundreds years now, is the electoral college. As in the case of the election of U.S. senators, the convention that framed and submitted the Constitution decided that the selection of the president should not be made directly by the people. Therefore, they provided that each state would choose presidential electors equal in number to the senators and representatives in the Congress from that state. This involved the creation of what they called the "Electoral College." It was the intent of the convention, as clearly shown by the debate, that the people could only choose the electors, who would then, with complete freedom of choice, select a president for them. This conception was short-lived. By the end of Washington's term, the people had divided themselves into two political parties: Federalist and Anti-Federalist. With the exception of one or two elections in which a third party was a substantial participant, the two-party system has prevailed to the present time. The electors relate to a given party and its "ticket."

By tradition, although not by law, presidential electors are pledged to vote for the candidates for president and vice president of the party they represent. Due to the fact that all the presidential electors from each state go to the candidate who carries that state, however small his margin, there has been one instance when the president chosen by the electoral college did not, in fact, receive a majority of the people's vote. There have also been one or two other occasions when the margin of popular vote was breathtakingly close, while the electoral vote did not reflect this closeness, but was substantially in favor of one candidate. Therefore, we have been faced with the fear that under the electoral-college system, it would be quite possible at any time for a candidate who succeeded in carrying, even by a scant margin, several of the larger states, to be elected even though his opponent had clearly won the popular vote of the nation. Because of this, Congress has many times striven to draft an amendment to the Constitution, to be submitted to the states, overhauling the machinery for electing the president and vice president.

Should the electoral college be abolished? The flash judgment of many, if not most, of our people is to discard it entirely, as a leftover from the early days of the republic when the people were intentionally denied the privilege to choose their president. Closer examination, however, reveals that the electoral college still performs a vital function, and if its defects can be cured, it should be retained.

The electoral college has long preserved the two-party system which has stabilized the nation. As long as the electoral vote of each state cannot be split into fragments, splinter parties, the bane of many a foreign parliament, cannot flourish here. Under direct elections, a dozen parties could nominate candidates. If only a plurality were required to elect, we could have presidents favored by only a minority of the voters. If a majority or even 40 percent were required, a runoff election between the two leading candidates would need to be provided for, which is almost unthinkable. The nation is kept in a constant upheaval long enough now, without superimposing a second election on the first.

Furthermore, the electoral college isolates corruption. If bundles of ballots are miscounted or destroyed in a large city, only the electoral vote of one state is affected. If the ballots of all the people were

dumped into one national pot, election frauds in a single metropolitan area could nullify the votes of several states. Thus, under the
electoral-college system, state lines are a safeguard, like fire partitions
in a building or watertight compartments in a ship. These are the
reasons Congress has many times refused to abolish the electoral
college.

Now, as in the past, two methods are offered to reform the electoral college. One, the so-called "proportional system," would split each
state's electoral vote into fractions proportionate to its popular vote.
But this method, like the direct election, opens the way for splinter
parties and runoff elections. The other method, the "district system,"
would permit each congressional district to choose one elector, and the
states to choose two electors-at-large, so each state's electors would total,
as now, its number of senators and representatives. In the past, this
method has been rejected because congressional districts, juggled and
gerrymandered by state legislatures, were glaringly unequal in population. But this inequality no longer exists. Under the "one man, one
vote" decision of the Supreme Court, legislatures have been compelled
to see to it that congressional districts contain, as nearly as practicable,
equal population. This, in my opinion, makes the district system as
near perfect as any that could be devised. It guards against splinter
parties and even further limits the effects of fraud and irregularities in
the congressional district in which they may occur. It gives every vote
the same weight, for each citizen would vote for one district elector
and two at-large for his state. No longer would a New Hampshire
citizen be voting for four electors, while his cousin in New York votes
for forty-five. In other words, since the Supreme Court has compelled
the balancing of congressional districts, the district system would preserve all the advantages of the present electoral-college system and
none of its defects. I suggest that this is the constitutional amendment
that should be submitted by the Congress and adopted by the states.

It is interesting to note, however, that some 44 times Congress
has debated and rejected such a district system. It has also rejected
the proportional system each time it has been proposed. Three times
in the early years it was seriously suggested that the president be

chosen from a selected group by drawing lots. The proponents of this absurd notion argued that it would save us from the excitement of elections, which, they said, "convulse the whole body politic." And in those days, they had never had to watch a national convention on television!

CHAPTER

XV

The Judicial Branch

We must remember that we have to make judges out of men, and that by being made judges their prejudices are not diminished and their intelligence is not increased.

—*Robert G. Ingersoll*

THE first lesson learned by every student of government, even in the rudimentary courses given in high school or earlier, is that the strength of the American constitutional democracy, as well as its hope for permanence, depends upon the separation of its executive, legislative, and judicial branches. I have already noted how, largely because of the growth of the nation and its leadership in the world, the powers of the presidency have increased. I have also dwelt on how, by broadening the commerce clause in the Constitution, the Congress has expanded its power to control the lives and activities of citizens, ever narrowing the powers once reserved to the states. Even though the main purpose of this narrative is to examine the Congress, a quick look at what has happened to the judicial branch of our government is in order. This is not really a digression, because the exercise of new powers by an activist Supreme Court has been a matter of deep concern in the Congress—the subject of much debate and even of some limiting legislation.

The framers of the Constitution clearly intended that the powers of the judicial branch should be more carefully circumscribed than those of the other two branches. One obvious reason for this restraint was that both the president and Congress are elected by the people

197

for fixed terms, at the end of which periods they can be replaced if for any reason the people disapprove of them or their performance of the duties of their office. The people have no direct voice in selecting the justices of the Supreme Court or other federal judges, for they are nominated by the president and confirmed by the Senate. Once in office, federal judges can only be removed by death, impeachment, or their own voluntary retirement.

Alexander Hamilton explained, with almost brutal candor, the limitations put upon the Court by the framers of the Constitution.

> The judiciary, from the nature of its functions, will always be the least dangerous to the political rights of the Constitution; because it will be least in a capacity to annoy or injure them . . . the judiciary . . . has no influence over either the sword or the purse; no direction either of the strength or of the wealth of the society; and can take no active resolution whatever. It may truly be said to have neither FORCE nor WILL, but merely judgment; and must ultimately depend upon the aid of the executive arm even for the efficacy of its judgments. . . . [It] is beyond comparison the weakest of the three departments of power; [and] can never attack with success either of the other two.

For a time, the Supreme Court abided by this concept. It delivered its judgments; but it depended upon the president to enforce them, and in some cases, where necessary, the Congress had to implement its judgments by enacting legislation before the executive could, in fact, enforce them. But even during the life of Chief Justice Marshall, the Supreme Court began to be restive under its restrictions. President Andrew Jackson promptly squelched, for the time being at least, any movement on the part of the Court to expand its powers. After the Court had decided a case between the states of Georgia and South Carolina, Jackson, in his usual brusque manner, said, "They have made their judgment; now let's see them enforce it."

Hamilton's interpretation of the constitutional power (or, rather, the lack of power) of the Supreme Court, was corroborated by his rival, Thomas Jefferson, who in 1825, in a letter to Edward Livingston, not only confirmed the restrictions upon the powers of the Court, but warned that it was exceeding those powers:

> This member of the government was at first considered as the most harmless and helpless of all its organs. But it has proved that the power of declaring what the law is, *ad libitum*, by sapping and mining, slyly, and without alarm, the foundations of the Constitution, can do what open force would not dare to attempt.

Jefferson might have been apprehensive, indeed, if he could have foreseen the lengths to which the Supreme Court would go in later years, particularly in the 1960s, in encroaching upon the prerogatives of both the executive and legislative branches of the government.

Whether there were some slight and isolated incursions during the many years that elapsed between the death of Chief Justice Marshall and the advent of Chief Justice Warren, I cannot say. That would require extensive research to determine. One can state, however, without fear of contradiction, that the first real invasion by the Supreme Court of what had previously been considered the exclusive domain of the executive and legislative branches came under the leadership of Earl Warren, as chief justice of the United States, and was in connection with the decision of the Court in the case of *Brown* v. *Board of Education*, compelling school integration. (Incidentally, I have never faulted the Warren Court for that decision; I commend them for it. It rectified a long-standing injustice to the black race. I never believed in the doctrine of "separate-but-equal" facilities. Through the years, the white and black schools certainly were separate, but never equal. Indeed, the Warren Court rendered a real service when it placed the final seal of approval upon several social reforms. It has been well stated that the Constitution is a living document—flexible enough to be capable of application to the changing needs of society.)

Although the Supreme Court's decision in the Brown case was sound and just, the Court then embarked upon a virtually unprecedented and, in my opinion at least, a dangerous course when it sought to implement and enforce its own decision. This decision, the first long step toward integration of the races, was far-reaching, not only reversing what had been the fundamental law of the land, but radically changing long-established customs in many states. This the Court clearly recognized and set forth in the text of its decision. It further recognized that reasonable time must be allowed for states and communities to conform. This was acknowledged when the Court declared changes should be made with "all deliberate speed." However, the Court did not afford the Congress an opportunity to implement this epic-making decision by appropriate legislation, although Congress proved its willingness to do so by passing four strong civil-rights enforcement bills. The Supreme Court did not afford the president the opportunity to execute the law as interpreted and articulated by the Court, although he proved his willingness to do so by sending paratroopers to Little Rock to protect the process of integrating the schools, as he sent forces elsewhere for the same purpose. Instead, the Court dispatched enforcement officers of the federal courts, namely U.S. marshals, to implement and enforce its decisions.

Conceivably an attempt by the Supreme Court to take over the enforcement of its own decisions could be justified as a last resort, if the president declined to enforce them, if the Congress failed to implement them when necessary, or if states refused to be bound by them. However, such an instance probably has not occurred since the period of Andrew Jackson. Even the hated Dred Scott decision was reluctantly enforced by the northern states. Certainly, no such defiance of a Supreme Court decision has happened in recent years. On the contrary, I can testify that in the long debates which took place in the Senate following the Brown decision, southern senators, while admitting frankly that they disagreed with the Court's decision and, in some cases, that they could not personally accept racial equality, declared that the decision of the Supreme Court was the law of the land and, therefore, their states must and would comply. While I was still sitting on the Judiciary Committee, which dealt with many of these problems, we had governors come before us opposing certain provisions in civil-rights bills, but not one of them ever asserted that the decision of the Court as implemented by legislation would be defied or disobeyed in his state.

In light of the years, Hamilton's use of the word "weakest" in referring to the judicial branch has proven to be an overstatement. Not only are the opinions rendered by the Supreme Court almost universally accepted and obeyed, the Court also enjoys complete immunity from many of the assaults that are made upon the other branches and is guarded and protected in its right to determine the ultimate law, unhampered by outside influences or pressures of any nature.

Of course, as I have noted, the federal judiciary is not subject to the elective process, but more than that, it is not even accessible to the general public. A citizen may approach his senator or congressman, petition him, lobby him, even threaten him. Labor unions, business associations, organizations for or against gun control or abortions or women's rights may inveigh against the president, picket the White House, and are frequently admitted to the chief executive's presence. But the Supreme Court is immune to all this.

In this volume, I have been able to recount pleasant, sometimes comic, occasionally critical anecdotes and personal experiences relating to fellow senators and to presidents with whom I have had contact. This I cannot do in the case of the Supreme Court, and for good reason. As a member of the Senate, I had no personal contact with any of the justices, and in a sense was not permitted to know them. Sometimes a brash, inexperienced young representative, or even a senator, has sought an interview with a member of the Supreme Court. He has invariably received the polite brush-off, unless he made it perfectly clear that his errand was completely personal. (I recall an instance when one of my friends in the Senate, who used a hearing aid, learned that a Supreme Court justice, who was similarly afflicted, was extremely dissatisfied with his. He reached the judge on the telephone and asked to see him briefly. The judge, in rather frosty tones, demanded to know what he wished to discuss with him. My friend explained that he merely wanted to show him his type of hearing aid, which he thought the judge would find much more effective. The justice then thawed in his attitude and laughed heartily. He invited the senator to his office, thanking him for his thoughtfulness, and saying, "I guess there cannot be anything improper in your trying to influence me in the choice of a hearing aid.")

It is not difficult to understand why justices of the Supreme Court would shy away from interviews with members of the U.S. Senate. Even if a member of the legislative branch were not seeking to discuss a case pending before the Court, any general discussion could concern issues which the Court might later have to decide. Oh, I suppose that a few senior members of Congress, who are in their own right eminent lawyers and who are perhaps chairmen or high-ranking members on the Judiciary Committee of either the Senate or the House, may have, by invitation, conferred with the justices. Of that, I would not know. Typically, however, justices of the Court do not frequent social events or cocktail parties where they might find themselves rubbing elbows not only with members of the legislative and executive branches, but with Washington lobbyists, who abound at such functions. From much of the general social life of the capital, they properly hold themselves aloof.

Far from being weak, the Supreme Court has acquired awesome power, which can even become dangerous at times. Indeed, the Warren Court, in its solicitude for the rights of the alleged criminal, in decisions such as the Mallory and Miranda cases, set up roadblocks making it extremely difficult, if not virtually impossible, to convict perpetrators of the most violent crimes, thus unleashing dangerous elements in our society. It assumed for itself powers delegated by the Constitution to the Congress, the president, and the states, thus moving government away from those elected and controlled by the people, to those appointed for life and beyond the people's reach. During that period, the Court did not hesitate to interfere with state legislatures and local elections.

Long before the advent of Chief Justice Warren and some of his rather freewheeling associate justices, the Supreme Court had stretched to the fullest extent its power to interpret laws passed by the Congress. When I was a student in law school in Washington, retired

Chief Justice William Howard Taft, though in failing health, consented to give one lecture to the combined student bodies of several law schools in the city. In his characteristically humorous vein, he remarked that any person sitting in the galleries of the House or Senate during a particularly stormy debate over the passage of some bill might be amazed if he could later see the members of the Supreme Court "quietly deciding what the lawmakers meant—if they meant anything." But the Warren Court went even beyond that. Previously, if the constitutionality of an act of Congress was taken to the Supreme Court, the Court either upheld it as constitutional or found it to be unconstitutional and nullified it (leading, perhaps, to congressional passage of a modified version). The Warren Court, however, in one instance at least, did neither; it proceeded to amend the law as passed by Congress.

Being only a former country lawyer, I would not venture to analyze, much less attack, the long chain of landmark decisions made by the Warren Court. I can, however, refer to the bitter dissent on the part of some of the ablest members of the Court, several of them with liberal backgrounds. Justice Cardozo cried out that although justice is due the lawbreaker, it is due to the law abider as well. Justice Stewart ridiculed the notion that a religion was being established if children, before drinking their milk, were permitted to say an innocuous prayer. Frankfurter, a great judge and a great liberal, was shocked at the Warren Court's trying to decide who shall sit in state legislatures, saying, "Such a political conception . . . is to rewrite the Constitution." Harlan and White were equally shocked when, after the Congress had stormed and fought for many weeks and passed an open-housing law, the Court calmly amended it.

Mr. Justice Jackson, another liberal, at a time when the Court had only started on its binge to make good guys out of criminals and bad guys out of police, said, "Unless the Court starts to temper its doctrine with logic and a little bit of common sense, you are going to turn the Bill of Rights into a suicide pact."

Richard Nixon's fatal error in attempting to conceal the truth about Watergate has caused the public to forget some of the good accomplishments of his administration. Perhaps one of the greatest of these was the fact that he restored for us a reasonably balanced Supreme Court. Possibly if he had been permitted to have his own way, we would now have a Court that leaned too far to the right, as the Warren Court did to the left. But the Senate refused to confirm the nominations of Haynsworth and Carswell, resulting in the appointment of a more moderate conservative—which proves that our system of appointing and confirmation is, in the main, an effective one. In Chief Justice Burger, President Nixon found a judge who certainly is not a hidebound conservative, but who apparently has no intention of leading the Supreme Court on crusades or causing it to seek to usurp the functions of either the executive or the Congress. That the Supreme Court is still somewhat too liberal was shown, I think, when it recently, in a five-to-four decision, set aside a state statute imposing mandatory death for killing a police officer. The majority ruled that such things as the youth of the offender, absence of prior convictions, the influence of drugs or alcohol, and "even the existence of circumstances which the offender reasonably believed provided moral justification for his conduct" (whatever that last may mean) must be taken into consideration. That decision further endangers the life of every policeman who dares to enter a dark alley at night. (Justices Rehnquist and White, on the other hand, as two of the four dissenters, said state law should make it "unmistakably clear [that] punishment in the form of death will be inexorable" for police slayers.) Much as this particular decision disturbs me, I still think it can be truly said that we now appear to have a reasonably balanced Supreme Court, performing the functions intended by the framers of the Constitution.

Back in the 1830s, the French statesman de Tocqueville, in his book *Democracy in America*, showed remarkable powers of prophecy: "The President, [with] limited power, may err without causing great mischief in the State. Congress may decide amiss without destroying the Union, because the [people may] retract its decision by changing its members. But if the Supreme Court is ever composed of imprudent men, or bad men, the Union may be plunged into anarchy or civil war."

Let us hope we have passed the point of greatest danger from excesses by the judicial branch of the government and are well on our way back to a moderate, reasonably balanced Supreme Court.

CHAPTER

XVI

Personal Decisions a Senator Must Make

Be ever careful in your choice of friends,
And let your special love be given to those
Whose strength of character may prove the whip
That drives you ever to fair Wisdom's goal.

—*Mutsuhito, Emperor of Japan*

PROBABLY one of the most distinguished careers in American history was that of James Francis Byrnes of South Carolina. Jimmy Byrnes served as a congressman, U.S. senator, justice of the Supreme Court, assistant to the president of the United States (perhaps the first person to be officially recognized as such), and as secretary of state. His last office was that of governor of his native state, South Carolina—which he regarded as the greatest post of them all, for to him (as to most born and bred southerners) the sovereignty of the states is almost a religion. Byrnes was possessed of one of the keenest, sharpest, and most agile minds of this or any other generation. He was recognized as one of the great lawyers of our time; he knew government and was aware of all the dangers and pitfalls that come with power; and, above all, having come up through the ranks the hard way (starting as a court reporter), he had a practical knowledge of human nature and knew the people, from the humblest to the highest.

Byrnes had a favorite story. He used to tell of the farmer who had acquired a new hand. The first day he sent him out to dig postholes, preparatory to fencing a large field. He was astonished when the young man returned by midafternoon, to report that the postholes surrounding the field were all dug. The next morning the farmer asked

207

him to start setting the posts and, if possible, to begin stringing the fence wire. To his delighted amazement, when milking time came, at the end of the day, the hired man reported that the posts were all set, the wire all strung, and the fence was completed. This seemed incredible, but the farmer went out, inspected, and found it to be true. He decided he had acquired a real gem, whom he must keep. So the next morning, which was rainy, he decided to give the young man an easier task. He took him into the basement and showed him a pile of last year's potatoes, saying, "All I want you to do is to sort these, throwing those that are starting to rot in one pile and the sound ones in another." Hardly an hour had elapsed before the young man came upstairs and asked the farmer to pay him off and give him his discharge. "I can't understand you," said the farmer. "The last two days you worked long and hard and performed wonders; and now when I give you something easy to do, you want to quit." "I don't mind hard work," replied the young man. "It's making decisions that wears me down."

Anyone seeking or holding any public office, from pound keeper to president, soon learns that the price one pays for political preferment is the necessity of constantly making decisions—decisions that sometimes affect one's whole political future. Nowhere, with the exception of the presidency, is the need for constant decision-making more burdensome than in the U.S. Senate.

In most cases, one who dares aspire to membership in the Senate finds himself up against his first painful decision when he has to conclude whether, at any given time, he should indeed make the attempt. In many cases, like my own, the person seeking a Senate seat is a member of the House and, having served several terms, is well entrenched, with what is called a "safe" seat. During his years in Washington, his professional practice or his established business at home has been neglected, so that if he runs and fails, his future and that of his family could be very bleak. Yet, when the opportunity arises, through the death or retirement of a senator from his state, he has the feeling that if he does not make the attempt then, he may spend the rest of his life wondering if he should not have done so. I often think that nowhere in life are those familiar words of Shakespeare more clearly exemplified:

> There is a tide in the affairs of men,
> Which, taken at the flood, leads on to fortune;
> Omitted, all the voyage of their life
> Is bound in shallows and in miseries.

As long as I live, I shall never forget my first desperate campaign for the Senate. It is so typical of situations that frequently occur in the hazardous game of politics that it seems worth recounting. When Senator Tobey died suddenly of a heart attack, Hugh Gregg was governor of New Hampshire. Under our state law, when a senator dies the governor appoints an interim senator to serve until the next regular election—in this case, it involved about a year's time. Governor Gregg appointed attorney Robert W. Upton of Concord to serve for this period. Robert Upton was one of the ablest men that New Hampshire ever produced. He was a recognized leader of the New Hampshire bar and had long been active in the councils of the Republican party, so much so that he was frequently referred to in the state as "Mr. Republican." Undoubtedly he could have been a senator years earlier, but his extensive law practice, as well as family and other responsibilities, prevented his devoting himself to public officeholding.

At the time of Upton's appointment, he was nearly, if not quite, seventy years of age. It was assumed, therefore, that the governor had named him merely to fill the interim and that the governor himself would seek the senatorship in the upcoming election. However, the death of Governor Gregg's brother and the advancing age of his father made it necessary for him to give up politics, for a time at least, and to devote himself exclusively to an extensive family manufacturing business. As soon as the governor made this known, Wesley Powell, later a governor of New Hampshire, announced his candidacy for the Republican nomination for the Senate. I interviewed Senator Upton, who had not yet determined his own course, and he said he would inform me when his decision was made as to whether he would run. Time passed and Powell, always a formidable and energetic candidate, was actively campaigning. Influential members of the party were of the opinion that Senator Upton would not be a candidate. They suggested that if I were ever to try for the Senate, now was the time and that I could not afford to delay. This became my opinion, too, and I announced my candidacy. Somewhat later, to my dismay, Upton announced his.

There was no issue that could be raised against Senator Upton, other than his age—and that I could not do, since such would have been both unfair and unfortunate, particularly in New Hampshire, which at that time had a higher percentage of elderly people than any other state except Florida. For me it was a hard and discouraging campaign. Upton, the incumbent by appointment, was highly respected and had the support of most of the bench and bar, as well as other older and solid elements in the party and the state's largest newspaper. I had strong support in my own congressional district, except for the city of Concord, where Upton resided; but I was little known in the eastern congressional district. As primary day approached, I became convinced I could not win. I well remember warning my wife on primary-election night, as we were driving to my state headquarters, that we must keep cheerful, show our appreciation to our friends, but be prepared for an unhappy evening which would very likely mark the end of my public service.

The early returns seemed to bear out my prediction. I ran a poor third in the state's largest city, Manchester, and in nearly all of the First Congressional District. But those areas were split between Upton and Powell, and my own congressional district, other than Concord, gave me such an overwhelming vote that I won by a plurality—which under our state law was sufficient. (It is interesting to note, in view of my earlier comments on the Seventeenth Amendment, that had the selection of senators remained in the legislature or had our law provided for a runoff primary, Senator Upton would very likely have been victorious.) Then, in the general election, I went on to defeat my Democratic opponent without difficulty.

Such are the hazards and uncertainties of politics. In the years since, I have seen many able and influential members of the House make the decision to take a similar plunge for the Senate, only to find themselves relegated to private life. Some have been as fortunate as I was back in 1954, but it is a precarious course—and a fateful decision to make.

It almost goes without saying that if one succeeds in being elected to the Senate, one is immediately faced with all kinds of decisions, major and minor. These continue to arise as long as one remains in the Senate, whether it be for a brief time or for many years. Of course, a senator has to make a decision every time he votes on any bill. Such legislative decisions are part of the job of being a senator. A particular thing about them that a senator sometimes must learn from experience is that one cannot straddle a vexing issue. It is impossible to please everyone, and a senator is likely to find himself in trouble if he makes the attempt. I often think of how Alben Barkley used to lecture freshmen senators on this point with his favorite admonition: "Remember, you can't be noble and nimble at the same time."

But voting decisions were not what I really had in mind to discuss. There are other judgments that have to be made which may have much to do with shaping one's entire career in the Senate. First is the selection of a staff. The effectiveness of a senator, not only in serving his constituents, but in making his mark in the Senate, depends in no small degree on the ability and efficiency of his staff. Of course, if he has served previously in the House, he already has the nucleus of a staff and, more important, has learned what qualities to seek in making his selections and how his office organization should be balanced. If he comes into the Senate directly from private life, he often has to learn this the hard way.

It is important to proportion an office force between people from the senator's home state and others who are seasoned by years of experience on Capitol Hill. Handling the routine of a senatorial office, dealing with committees and the staffs of other members, as well as with the many executive departments downtown, has become a profession in itself. A reasonable number of experienced staffers are necessary to orient the aides a senator recruits from home (and to a certain degree, the senator himself) to the intricacies of the federal government. On the other hand, those new ones the senator brings with him will have some firsthand knowledge about the people he represents.

The most difficult decision in this connection is in choosing an administrative assistant with the executive ability required to supervise the senator's entire staff, both in Washington and at home. If such a person can be found, he can relieve the senator of having to cope with the minor frictions that are bound to develop. The person selected for this important post can be either from the home state or someone with previous experience on the Hill, provided he or she has the necessary competence.

Another important decision which should be made at the outset is for what committee or committees the senator wishes to aim. Probably he will not attain them at first, but if his desires are known and he persists, he is likely to get the assignments he wants sooner than would otherwise be achieved.

In my opinion, the most important decision, by far, that a senator should make very early in his service, and make with care, is whom he chooses for friends, both among his colleagues on the Hill and within the Washington community. It is almost inevitable that in the years ahead he will be influenced by these early associations. This does not mean that he should turn his back on anybody, but it does mean that he should from the beginning take careful thought and exercise discretion in choosing those in whom he puts his trust. A considerable number of members of both houses of Congress have found their reputations tarnished in recent times by conduct that, if not illegal, has been regarded as unethical. The explanation most often advanced for behavior that has brought the Congress in disrepute is that times have changed and that since Watergate a new and higher code of ethics has come into being, so that practices which in the past were considered entirely proper are now frowned upon. This is not valid. The Watergate exposures did not bring about a new set of ethical standards, they merely put the spotlight of publicity on practices that had been going on for years, but which had received little attention from the public because they had not been greatly emphasized by the press. Long before Watergate, campaign funds had been heedlessly intermingled, if not actually misappropriated, by candidates. Over the years there were members who had used their franking privilege for other than official business—members who habitually took junkets all over the world, without any real legislative purpose, enjoying luxuries at public expense—members who unhesitatingly accepted, even solicited, from labor, business, and other groups large honorariums for making speeches—and members who brazenly called on lobbyists to provide food and liquid refreshment for their own private parties.

True, some of these practices (for instance, securing private planes, belonging to corporations, to transport senators to attend and speak at political functions) were not formerly considered improper. It is also true that practices which were clearly wrong, as well as ones of questionable propriety, have long existed and that substantial numbers of both branches of Congress have been guilty of them.

It has been my observation that, in many cases, members have fallen into bad habits because, at the outset of their service, they developed associations with colleagues who not only lacked deep-seated scruples regarding the acceptance of favors and gifts, but who seemed to be dedicated to the belief that the holding of high office entitled them to special privileges and rewards. I consider the choice of friends to be the most important decision a newcomer to either house of the Congress must make. That is why, at the head of this chapter, I quote the admonition "Be ever careful in your choice of friends. . . ."

Another decision which new senators are frequently forced to make may in the long run prove very embarrassing. The Senate, particularly in recent years, has been constantly crumbling into factions, alliances, and coalitions. The public is prone to have the impression that the Senate is engrossed in a continual struggle between the two political parties. The formal and traditional organization of the Senate might seem to support this impression. Senators win their election as either Democrats or Republicans; each party occupies its own side of the Senate, with the center aisle dividing them; each party has its own cloakroom and its own private dining room, assigns its members to committees, holds its own caucuses and conferences, elects its own leadership, and has its own system of seniority and the administration of its internal affairs. But when one acquires a more intimate knowledge of the actual workings of the Senate, one learns that this separation of the political parties is a matter of form rather than substance. The sharpest divisions and hardest contests are *not* along party lines.

As a matter of fact, the issues between the two political parties are so constantly changing—certain ones coming to the fore in particular campaigns, and then sinking into the background—that it is always difficult for a student of politics to give a clear-cut answer to the oft-repeated question, "What are the creeds of the two parties and in what do they differ?" Indeed, one almost has to resort to an historian's definition of the conflicting philosophies of the original founders of the two-party system, Hamilton and Jefferson: "Hamilton's chief concern was to safeguard and preserve the Ship of State. Jefferson was more interested in the welfare of the crew." Even this demarcation is somewhat blurred, because today both parties are concerned with the safety of the republic and with the welfare of its people. Nowadays, the differences and issues separating the two parties are more a matter of emphasis.

In the Congress the party of the president usually supports the administration and the other party opposes it—and much partisan rhetoric is always heard as a new election approaches. But many, if not all, of the real splits and the hard contests cut across party lines. Sometimes the battle is between sections: the agrarian portions of the South and the West against the industrial East. Sometimes it is the metropolitan centers against rural and suburban areas. But most of all, the strife is likely to be between liberals and conservatives—the liberals and conservatives of both political parties.

This rivalry manifests itself to almost every senator as soon as he enters the Senate. When each new Congress meets, both parties proceed to organize and choose their leadership. This occurs in executive (secret) sessions, so I have little knowledge of the Democrats' procedure. However, Republicans elect their floor leaders, the chairman of their Conference, the chairman of their Policy Committee, the chairman of the Committee on Committee Assignments, and the chairman of the Republican Senatorial Campaign Committee. Almost invariably there are two candidates for each of these positions—one a liberal and the other a conservative. Thus, each new senator (or senator-elect) at the very outset of his service, usually even before the Senate has had its first session and he has been sworn in, is forced to make a choice between individuals with whom, in most cases, he is hardly acquainted and of whose political philosophy he may be hardly aware. Now, within the Republican party in the Senate there are two organizations —the liberal "Wednesday Club" and the conservative "Steering Committee." Both of them are largely dominated by the hard-nosed extremists of each faction. (I believe there are similar organizations on the Democratic side.) The point is that if at the first meeting of the Senate Republicans a new senator happens to vote for most, if not all, of either the liberal or the conservative candidates, his political leanings are immediately assumed, at least to the extent of making him fair game to be solicited (and even pressured) to join either the liberal or the conservative group. He would be wise to think twice before doing so.

In the first place, these organized clubs within the party make it more difficult to secure reasonably united party action, which sometimes is very necessary if the two-party system is to be preserved. Furthermore, my years in the House and Senate have taught me that few members can be accurately pigeonholed, catalogued, or labeled as either liberal or conservative. Most people are conservative in some things and liberal in others. One may be conservative in domestic and fiscal policies, liberal in foreign relations and world trade, or vice versa. Only the extremists can be at peace with themselves if they bind themselves to groups carrying the banner of either faction.

There is another fact of life that militates against becoming involved with any extreme group. Decisions of political philosophy are often made for us, not by us. Winston Churchill once remarked that a man who is not a liberal in his twenties lacks compassion, and the man who is not a conservative in his fifties lacks common sense. I entered the Senate as a moderate liberal and cast my first vote to censure McCarthy; but in my latter years I found myself rated as a conservative. Yet, during that time, I had not altered my basic beliefs and principles. We are living in a fast-changing world. One may be progressive and liberal today but discover, twenty years hence, that public sentiment has surged so far ahead of one that, if you have kept your basic stance, you are rated as a conservative. I have watched this happen many, many times. The classic example I always remember is that of a great senator I observed when I was a young staffer with Senator Moses. Albert B. Cummins of Iowa had become known as one of that state's youngest and most popular governors. He had come to the Senate at the turn of the century as a Republican, but he was so liberal that he was frequently called a "Populist." For more than two decades, he was a towering figure in the Senate. Then, in the late twenties he was defeated by a radical member of the western farm bloc—a man who bore the appropriate name of Smith Wildman Brookhart. Cummins had not changed, but Iowa had. Today young liberals, even radicals, are defeating conservatives—but the conservatives they defeat were the liberals of yesterday.

(Parenthetically, I would like to comment upon the popular idea we hear advanced by so many these days, that it would be desirable for all the conservatives to be assembled in one of the major parties and all the liberals in the other. Proponents of this notion contend that such a realignment would separate the sheep from the goats and give the voter a real choice. In my estimation this concept is dead wrong, and for two reasons. First, as I have already noted, contrary to popular fancy, few individuals fully conform to either of these categories. Second, herding all those inclined to be liberal into one party and those of conservative bent into the other would be a disaster, for whenever a change of administration took place the whole fabric of government would be uprooted and torn asunder, almost to the point of chaos. A political party is an organization for government. Undoubtedly, the Republican party is somewhat to the right of center, and the Democrats somewhat to the left. However, each party should be leavened by including both those of conservative and liberal tendencies, so that when it is in power it can function reasonably and with restraint, without the nation falling into the hands of extremists.)

Whenever I see an instance of changing times overtaking a senator, I usually think of a perfect illustrative story. A somewhat aged farmer and his wife were driving into town in their Model T Ford. He sat clutching the wheel and smoking his pipe. She was seated in the extreme right corner of the seat, away from him. She suddenly remarked, "Forty years ago, when we were first married, we used to sit closer together." The old man, not taking his eyes from the road or missing a puff on his pipe, parried that observation in just three words. "*I* ain't moved," he said.

To some senators there eventually comes the final and most agonizing decision of them all. That will be the subject of my next and concluding chapter.

CHAPTER

XVII

Journey's End

Live your life, do your work, then take your hat.
—*Henry David Thoreau*

I HAVE come to believe that "agonizing" is one of the most overused words in the English language. Perhaps I feel so because senators and congressmen have used it so much in describing their decisions—particularly to constituents unhappy with their votes—and often on relatively unimportant measures. But when one who has served many years in the U.S. Senate reaches the age when he must face the prospect of voluntary retirement, that may truly be described as an "agonizing" decision.

The sadness of retirement is by no means confined to the Senate. We are living in a day when medical science has prolonged the life of many, while at the same time the brisk efficiency of the modern business, industrial, and professional world dooms them to spend their last years in idleness and frustration. During my years in public life, I have had occasion to attend many farewell testimonials for men and women reaching retirement. I have listened to the tributes and witnessed the presentation of watches, television sets, golf clubs, and hunting and fishing equipment. I have seen the apparently happy smiles on the faces of the recipients, and with the thoughtlessness of the younger generation, I have failed to see the heartache beneath. One never senses that until one's own time comes. No, there is nothing unique about retirement from the Senate, except that service there, despite the grueling campaigns for reelection and all the other headaches, is intense and exciting, and each year widens one's knowledge and increases one's influence. The very thought of leaving for the last time the familiar scenes of the chamber which have encompassed the best years of one's life is appalling. To make that decision requires all the will power one can possibly muster.

And so, at seventy-three, with the prospect of facing reelection the following year, my time of decision came. There were plenty of reasons that could have been advanced to rationalize my seeking yet another term—and, certainly, I thought of them all. I was vigorous and felt able to perform my duties with much the same zest as in the past. Experience and seniority had placed me in a position to accomplish more for New Hampshire and to exert a greater influence, generally, than ever before. At the beginning of the Ninety-third Congress, I had been elected chairman of the Republican Conference, and if reelected, I would have become the second-ranking Republican in the whole Senate, continuing as top minority member on the Commerce Committee and third on the Appropriations Committee. After nearly three decades in the Congress it would be hard to relinquish all this and retire, to rust on the shelf. But there was another side to the picture, and factors that, if faced squarely, led to an inescapable conclusion.

My wife was in a nursing home and needed my constant companionship, for we have no children. An even more important consideration, however, was the fact that I would have been eighty years old by the time I had served another six-year term, and my mind dwelt on some of the able and outstanding senators I had seen stay a little too long—senators like Theodore Francis Green of Rhode Island, who was still serving at ninety-two, and Carl Hayden of Arizona, at ninety-one. For years they had been powerful leaders in the Senate, but toward the last we had watched them totter about the floor, and sometimes fall asleep in their seats, having to be awakened by pages because of the impression given to observers in the galleries.

There is a time for coming and a time for going, and I was resolved not to let the infirmities and disabilities of old age overtake me while I still had the responsibilities of representing New Hampshire in the Senate. I owed that, surely, to the people who had elected me four times to the House and four times to the Senate. Therefore, sadly and reluctantly, I announced that I would not be a candidate for another term.

Frankly, it was not only the necessary decision, it was the sensible one. There is an old political adage: "Quit while you're ahead." Too many senators who have been victorious in many campaigns, and who have held their seats for many years, come to think of themselves as unbeatable. Not a few have ended a long and bright record in the gloom of defeat. I might well have won another term, because I always have "run scared" and campaigned hard. However, the matter of my age would have been raised against me. Indeed, in my last campaign for reelection, at the age of sixty-eight, my opponent, in the press and on the stump, insisted that New Hampshire could not afford "an old, tired, worn-out senator." My only answer to that was to tell one of my favorite stories, dedicating it to my opponent.

Three eighty-year-olds were basking in the sun at St. Petersburg, Florida. Somehow the conversation got onto the rather morbid subject of where they would prefer to be buried. One of them said, "I still believe in patriotism, and I wish I could be buried near the grave of that greatest of American patriots, Nathan Hale, who uttered those immortal words, 'My sole regret is that I have but one life to give for my country.'" The second said, "I'm an admirer of our martyred president, John F. Kennedy. I wish I were eligible to be buried in Arlington National Cemetary and could lie within sight of the eternal flame that burns by his grave." The third made no comment, whereupon one of them said, "Where would you prefer to be buried?" After a moment's thought, he replied, "I guess I would like to be buried next to Elizabeth Taylor." "But she ain't dead," exclaimed one of his friends. His reply: "AND NEITHER AM I."

Just as one learns many practical political lessons in the long struggle to reach the Senate, one learns a few much more quickly in preparing to leave. Partly out of consideration for potential candidates for my seat, but more to give the people of New Hampshire full opportunity to decide upon my successor, I revealed my decision a year before the upcoming election and a year and a half before my term was to expire. Immediately, I discovered a fact which I should perhaps have realized before: a senator's power and usefulness does not last until his term expires, or even until his successor is selected, but in many respects it comes to an abrupt end when he makes it known that he intends to step down.

Any real accomplishments that a senator is able to make, whether in promoting or opposing legislation, or in helping his state or his individual constituents, depend in a large measure on the good will and cooperation of his fellow senators. It is only human that members of the Senate, every one of whom has his own ax to grind, are less likely to go out of their way to cooperate with a colleague if they know he is not going to be around to return the favor. It is amazing how quickly and completely a retiring senator is made aware of his changed status. Whenever he attends a session of one of his committees or when he enters and takes his seat in the Senate chamber, he is greeted with unusual cordiality by his colleagues—but there is something strained and unnatural about the warmth exhibited toward him. (It somewhat resembles the solicitude we show toward those afflicted with a fatal illness.) There is a tendency to greet him with an almost exaggerated tenderness—and then, to a degree, avoid him. In the same way, a retiring senator receives special attention, even from those with whom his past associations have been rather casual. He is frequently referred to and eulogized upon the floor, but gradually he ceases to be included in the informal consultations which constantly take place.

Of course, there are exceptions. I well remember the last meeting of my Appropriations Subcommittee on Health, Education and Welfare, when we "marked up" the appropriations bill for the following year. Near the conclusion of the session, the chairman, Warren Magnuson, said, "Norris, who has served with us on this subcommittee for sixteen years, is not returning next year. Some of us feel that it would be appropriate to give his constituents a going-away present in this bill. Norris, what would you like for them?" Without hesitation I said, "Some more money for my pet project, the cancer center at Mary Hitchcock Memorial Hospital in Hanover, New Hampshire." They immediately voted five million dollars for that purpose. (Unfortunately, the president later insisted on an across-the-board cut of 10 percent on all the appropriations in the bill, before he would sign it, so the cancer center actually received four-and-a-half million dollars.)

Nevertheless, the overall effect of a senator's announcement of retirement is to impair greatly his influence. In light of my experience, I would advise any senator who has acquired membership on powerful committees and attained seniority in the Senate, to keep his own counsel and wait until the last possible minute before disclosing his intention to retire. He would do well to retain his maximum usefulness to those whom he represents, and to let prospective candidates take their own chances.

Another thing a senator learns upon announcing his retirement is that everyone in his state has always supported him. Indeed, he begins to be so puzzled by remembering the records that indicate the many thousands who voted against him in each of his campaigns, that he almost wishes he could obtain a recount.

The final separation from the familiar scenes and many associations in Washington is bound to be painful. As the date of my leaving drew near, I made a valiant attempt to concentrate on the many details incidental to pulling up stakes (the disposition of books and souvenirs accumulated over the years, the business decisions concerning my retirement allowance and what portion of it should be reserved for my wife in case I predeceased her, the seeking of placement for members of my staff who wished to continue on Capitol Hill . . .). In fact, I busied myself doing everything except selecting my coffin and making funeral arrangements. But, I must say, it did not work; I still found myself caught up in the emotions of leave-taking. My staff, all of whom were my loyal friends and many of whom had been with me for years and were retiring at the same time, insisted upon a farewell party. I had to bid goodbye to friends on committee staffs, in the departments downtown, and at the White House, as well as to some of the veteran newspapermen and lobbyists I had known so long. On the day of my departure, I had to make a final visit to the Senate, where, according to custom, I was invited to preside for a few minutes, before I went about the chamber shaking hands with colleagues of many years. There is a finality about all this to which one cannot close his mind, no matter how hard he tries. Flying out from Washington's National Airport makes it worse. As one takes to the air and soars over the city, he sees before his eyes the landmarks he has regarded so many times in returning for each new session of Congress—the Capitol, the Senate and House office buildings, the Mall, Washington Monument, the Lincoln and Jefferson Memorials, the White House. One realizes that he may see them again, but nevermore as a U.S. senator—never thereafter as an actor in the great drama that is the backdrop for life in the nation's capital.

Curiously, however (although I had no inkling of it then), I was destined to have a unique experience; there was to be an epilogue to my career in the Senate. The campaign to choose my successor resulted in the closest Senate race in the history of the United States. The regular election in New Hampshire on November 5 was not the end, but only the beginning, of the bizarre contest between Congressman Louis Wyman and his Democratic challenger, John Durkin. Mr. Wyman went to bed in the wee hours of the morning following the election, believing himself to be the winner by a margin of 355 votes (this according to the compilation of the news media). Naturally, a recount was called for by Mr. Durkin, and it was conducted under the direction of New Hampshire's secretary of state, in accordance with the state's law.

The recount resulted in Mr. Durkin's being declared the winner— by ten votes. Mr. Wyman, in turn, appealed to the New Hampshire Ballot Law Commission, which is empowered to inspect and pass upon the validity of contested ballots. This resulted in Wyman's being declared the winner by a margin of just *two* votes, out of the more than 223,000 cast.

The battleground then spread to the New Hampshire Superior and Supreme Courts, to the U.S. District Court, to the U.S. Court of Appeals, and on, finally, to the U.S. Senate itself—without having been resolved. (The dispute could not be taken to the Supreme Court of the United States because of the constitutional provision that the Senate and House shall be the final arbiters of the elections of their own members.) The contest is, and probably will ever remain, a land-mark in the political annals of the nation.

The Senate, contrary to past custom, refused to seat provisionally the state-certified winner, so that until the result was determined, New Hampshire had but one senator; and the contest dragged on week after week with no end in sight. The Senate Rules Committee set an all-time record for length of deliberation on one subject. The full Senate set a record with six unsuccessful attempts to vote cloture and limit debate. (The many facets of this now famous controversy are excellently and objectively set forth in a book by Donn Tibbetts, a New Hampshire reporter, who was perhaps the only person, other than the contestants and their counsel, to follow this battle in detail from its inception to its ultimate conclusion.)

As the weeks lengthened into months, the New Hampshire pro-tests against the unprecedented circumstance of the Senate's depriving a state of its constitutional right to be represented by *two* senators caught fire and became nationwide. Editorial writers and newscasters united in the demand that the Senate require a runoff election in New Hampshire, to fill the disputed seat, and that, in the meantime, the state be accorded the privilege of appointing a senator to serve until his successor be chosen and sworn in. This course had been advocated by candidate Wyman, but opposed by candidate Durkin. Ultimately, however, Durkin joined in the request. At that point, the Senate at last took action, declaring the seat vacant and authorizing New Hampshire's governor to call a special election between certain dates and, in the meantime, to appoint an interim senator to serve until his successor was seated. Governor Thomson set the election for September 16, and he named me to serve during the interim period.

Thus it was that I once again signed the Senate roster and went back on the rolls (and off retirement), as of August 8. I was not, however, formally sworn in by Vice President Rockefeller until the Senate reassembled after the Labor Day recess, and my actual participation in the activities of the Senate lasted only from September 2 to September 18. I have referred to this period as my "epilogue," and it was indeed a strange experience.

Occasionally, I have seen senators who had served some years and then been defeated, subsequently achieve election and return to the Senate. They lost the seniority they had previously acquired, but they did not start at the bottom, because new senators invariably came in with them and their previous service caused them to outrank the utter newcomers. Not infrequently, senators have died in office and interim senators have been appointed to serve until the next regular election. These had to start from scratch, but although they were usually persons of distinction in their own states, they had no previous Senate service. I doubt really, however, if anyone else has ever served for twenty years in the Senate and then returned as the junior-most member of the whole body. My reduced status as the "100th senator" in seniority did not bother me, and I enjoyed being associated again with old friends. But there were, I must confess, a few circumstances that could have been annoying—if they had not been so amusing.

I was assigned an office that was just as far as one could possibly get from the Senate chamber and still be on Capitol Hill. This would have presented no particular difficulty had it not been for the fact that if the bells rang for a roll-call vote when I was in my office, it was physically impossible for me to get to the floor in time to vote; and after all the uproar that had taken place because New Hampshire had been deprived of its second senator, I did not want the news to go back home that their interim senator was not voting. This problem was ingeniously resolved by the superintendent of the building. To get to the Senate, I first had to journey around three sides of the huge office building, before taking the elevator to the basement, where I could catch a subway car to the Capitol. Perhaps an Olympic runner could have made it, but at my age it was impossible. However, the fourth side of the building, which led directly from my office to the corner where one descended to the subway, was occupied by the Capitol telephone exchange, an area which was locked against intruders. The superintendent very kindly gave me a key to this area, so that when the bells rang for a vote, all I had to do was unlock a door, gallop by about eighty astonished switchboard operators, pass through the door at the other end (which, of course, could be opened from the inside), and I was well on my way to the Senate chamber.

I would have been assigned the end seat of the last row in the extreme corner of the Senate chamber, had it not been for my old friend John Tower of Texas. Before my arrival and without my knowledge, he had the sergeant-at-arms put my nameplate on his desk and his affixed to the remote corner desk. When I discovered this I begged him to keep his own seat, telling him I could endure sitting in the back corner, since I would be there less than three weeks. But, graciously, he insisted, and I shall always remember his kindness.

I do not even recall my committee assignments. I did not bother to attend any committee sessions, for there was no sense in my listening to witnesses testifying about matters which would not be acted upon until I had gone. A few fairly important votes did take place, and I made it a point to inform myself regarding them, by reading the committee reports and discussing them with members of the committees that had listened to the evidence. That is all I did during the brief days of my reincarnation as a senator—and all I could do.

The circumstances of my second departure from the Senate are rather interesting. John Durkin had been overwhelmingly elected in the special election and was expected to arrive in Washington on September 18 to take the oath of office. My intention was that on the day before his arrival I would "fold up my tent, like the Arabs, and quietly steal away." However, Mike Mansfield, the majority leader and an old friend, came to me and suggested that, in view of the bitterness which had been engendered by the long controversy, it would be a gracious act for me to remain through the day on the eighteenth, preside over the Senate, and administer the oath to Senator-elect Durkin. This I was perfectly willing to do, but it required a little manipulating. Senator Mansfield arranged for the vice president to inform the president pro tempore that he would be necessarily absent on that day. He then arranged for the president pro tempore, Senator Eastland, to write me a letter saying that he, too, had to be absent, and asking me to preside over the Senate. That ensured my being in the chair at whatever time Mr. Durkin put in his appearance. There was one other slight complication. The moment Durkin finished repeating the oath of office, I would cease to be a senator and would not properly be in the chair. Therefore, Mansfield arranged for a senator to stand on the rostrum behind me and immediately receive the gavel.

When Durkin arrived, I directed the clerk to read his certification of election, and I then requested him to approach the chair. He did so, escorted by Senator McIntyre. I then rapped the Senate to its feet, as is the custom, administered the oath, which Senator Durkin repeated phrase by phrase, and as quickly as possible after he uttered the closing words "So help me God," I thrust the gavel into the hands of the senator behind me, shook Durkin's hand, and left the rostrum. In spite of all this carefully staged performance, I believe that there were a few instants when New Hampshire had *three* senators. The whole episode is an example of some of the elaborate formalities still practiced in the Senate.

I have mentioned that there are two lessons—at least—which can only be learned by a senator after he retires. The first lesson is that an ex-senator would be wise to keep away from Washington and resist the impulse to visit the Senate. My brief return by appointment brought this home to me in no uncertain manner. Some ten months earlier, I had severed my ties and returned home. There followed an extremely difficult period of readjustment. Christmas and New Year's passed easily enough, for I had always been at my home on those occasions. Then came the convening of a new Congress. On the television screen I watched the assemblying in the House chamber of the Senate and House, as well as the cabinet, the Supreme Court, and the Diplomatic Corps; and I saw the president of the United States escorted to the rostrum to deliver his annual message on the State of the Union. For twenty-eight years, ever since I had gone to Washington as a freshman congressman, I had never missed one of those occasions. During recent years, as one of the leadership, I had been named to the committee to conduct the president into the chamber, thus being an active participant in the traditional ceremonies at the opening of Congress.

It was then, and not until then, that the full force of my retirement hit me.

The weeks that followed were lonely and dismal. It was hard to break the habit of nearly thirty years, and subconsciously, I was always half expecting I would be returning to Washington the following Monday, to attend committee meetings and answer roll calls. It was months before I was able to adjust myself to a life of retirement and to develop a measure of contentment. Then, because of my interim appointment, I returned to the familiar atmosphere of the Senate and for a period of days mingled once again with my colleagues on the floor, in the cloakrooms, at lunch, and in caucuses and conferences. That undid all I had accomplished in nearly a year at home. It rekindled all my longings to be back in the fray; indeed, it was much like the case of a reformed alcoholic who takes another drink.

When I left the Senate for a second time and came home, I had to start my period of adjustment all over again. It was then that I finally learned my lesson and resolved that a long, long time must elapse, or some extraordinary circumstances occur, before I would ever revisit the Capitol. All Senate retirees may not necessarily share this reaction. Temperaments differ. Some former members remain in Washington and frequent the floor of the Senate, but most of my friends who have retired tell me they have reached the same conclusion I have, and I strongly suspect that many who cannot bring themselves to leave the capital are eating their hearts out because they are on the outside looking in.

Another lesson that an ex-senator, returned home after long service to live out his days in retirement, soon learns is that he would be wise to make a determination as to the extent to which he will permit himself to become involved in political contests or in public controversies—and the sooner he makes that determination, and the more closely he adheres to it, the better.

In this connection, I was surprised to learn how few precedents there are, in New Hampshire at least, to aid one in making such a plan. In this century, only one New Hampshire senator other than myself has voluntarily retired after extended service. That was Henry W. Keyes, who back in the 1930s returned, in frail health, to his home in North Haverhill, and in the short time that he survived lived almost in seclusion, so he had no problems regarding his participation in public matters. The code of conduct to which I am referring would apply only to those of advanced years, who have retired after long service, and not to younger men who have been separated from the Senate.

I gave careful thought to what should be the stance of a retired fifty-year veteran who had held office in town, county, state, and national governments. Obviously, my own political career being ended, I had no further ambitions to fulfill and certainly no grudges to pay off. Clearly, I owed a certain degree of loyalty and support to the party under whose banner I had been elected to a long series of public offices, and in whose principles I believed—although I was also grateful for the support I had received (especially in the latter days of my service) from members of the other party and from independents. I became convinced that I should not be active in promoting the candidacies of individuals, for I question the right of anyone to make use of such prestige as may have accrued to him as a long-time senator, supported by many different groups and factions, to promote the cause of any one individual or single group. And certainly it would be presumptious to attempt to dictate to friends who had been loyal through the years just whom they should support.

My experience in observing the roles which have, over the years, been played by retired senators convinces me that the activity in which they should exercise the most careful restraint—and that in which they most frequently fail to do so—is in the use of their tongues. Seasoned by years in public life and finding themselves on the shelf, they are constantly tempted to express themselves publicly on every issue that arises, until even their best friends cease to heed them. Two fundamental precepts can, if followed, save us oldsters from that error. First, one should refrain from criticizing one's successors in office. We had our opportunities and, even though we served faithfully, we cannot claim to have cured all the ills of government. We would do well, therefore, to give the next incumbent his chance and refrain from carping criticism. Second, and more important, although one is still a citizen, has had the advantage of long and practical experience, and is entitled to speak out on important pending issues when it seems necessary, one should be careful to do so with dignity, discretion, restraint—and not too often. This is the course I have laid down for myself and which I have tried to follow.

*   *   *

I can think of no greater privilege than the one granted me by the people of New Hampshire—service in the Senate of the United States. Its associations deepen and mellow as the years go by, and the greatest days were the latter days. I think of the words of Rollin Wells in his poem "Growing Older":

> A little more tired at the close of day,
> A little ~~more~~ anxious to have our way,
> A little less ready to scold and blame,
> A little more care of a brother's name;
> And so we are nearing the journey's end,
> When time and eternity meet and blend.

ERRATA

PP. 231   2d LINE OF QUOTE "MORE" SHOULD BE "LESS"

Index